THE
CONTEMPORARY
MUSLIM MOVEMENT
IN THE
PHILIPPINES

THE
CONTEMPORARY
MUSLIM MOVEMENT
IN THE
PHILIPPINES

WRITTEN BY
Cesar Adib Majul

MIZAN PRESS, BERKELEY

Library of Congress Cataloging in Publication Data

Majul, Cesar Adib.
   The contemporary Muslim movement in the Philippines.

   Bibliography: p.
   Includes index.
   1. Muslims—Philippines—Politics and government.
2. Philippines—politics and government—1973-
I. Title.
DS666.M8M35   1985   959.9'00882971   85-21519
ISBN 0-933782-16-0
ISBN 0-933782-17-9 (pbk.)

Designed by Kathy Springmeyer
Manufactured in the United States of America

CONTENTS

* * *

CHAPTER ONE

THE MUSLIM
FILIPINO GROUPS
* * *

A CERTAIN TYPE of social reform movement appears again and again in the history of Muslim peoples throughout the world. These movements have been characterized by at least three common signs: an increased awareness of Islam—a re-awakening—among the Muslims; their commitment to reshape the social, cultural, and political structures of their communities to reflect better the Islamic ideal; and their vigorous efforts to eliminate any forces—both internal and external—that have disrupted or threatened their society and the Islamic ideal. The fundamental purpose behind all these movements, then, has been to preserve the integrity of the *umma*, or Islamic community.

But each movement has been manifested in a different way; each has been determined by its own distinct historical, political, and geographical circumstances. To understand the current social movement among the Muslim Filipinos—in which they are seeking autonomy, self-definition as Muslims, and recognition throughout the country as a group of citizenry separate from but equal to other Filipinos—we must consider their Philippine as well as their Islamic heritage. We must know not only something about the ideology of Islam and its general religious and social precepts and institutions, but also something about the particular history of the Muslim Filipino groups and how it has interwoven with the national history of the Philippines, about ethnolinguistic similarities and differences among the groups, and about their social and cultural institutions. Further, we must know something about their relationship not only with Muslims elsewhere in the world but with the non-Muslim majority in their own country, who outnumber them by far.

What is often referred to broadly as the "Muslim movement in the Philippines" in truth comprises several movements. These various factions—including traditional Muslim leaders and old-style politicians, Muslim national associations, "moderates," the Moro National Liberation Front (the MNLF), and the separate factions even within it—differ from each other in leadership styles and strategies for achieving their goals. Some believe only in negotiating with the Philippine government; others believe that stronger pressure is needed. But their ultimate goals are very much alike.

In examining this current movement and the strife in which it has embroiled the Muslim Filipinos, we ought to ask what it is they truly want for themselves as Muslims rather than as Filipinos, as members of communities that are Muslim first rather than separate ethnolinguistic groups within a nation of Southeast Asia. Indeed, they ought to ask it of themselves and of each other: What do they want as Muslims? For ultimately, their common goals and aspirations, as determined by Islamic ideals, have shaped and will continue to shape their history—both their historic past and the history they are making now.

* * *

MUSLIMS CONSTITUTE THE second largest religious community in the Philippines, a predominantly Catholic country. There were at least 3 million Muslim Filipinos in 1975, or 7 percent of the country's total population of 42,070,600. They can be classified according to the twelve ethno-linguistic groups listed in the table below. This table does not include data for the Badjao, or seafaring Samal, who are professed Muslims. Nor does it include Muslims among the Subanon in Zamboanga, the Bukidnon in Bukidnon, nor the 10 thousand Muslim converts in Manila and Luzon. And hundreds if not thousands of Maranao and other Muslims originally from Mindanao and Sulu have migrated to Manila and its environs.

MUSLIM FILIPINO GROUPS

Group Name	Population (est. 1975)
Maguindanao	674,000
Maranao and Iranun	670,000
Tausug	492,000
Samal	202,000
Yakan	93,000
Jama Mapun	15,000
Palawan groups (Palawani and Molbog)	10,000
Kalagan	5,000
Kolibugan	4,000
Sangil	3,000

SOURCE: Data from Peter Gowing, *Muslim Filipinos— Heritage and Horizon*, 1979, p. 2.

The vast majority of Muslims, however, live in the Philippine South, that is, on the island of Mindanao and in the Sulu Archipelago. The Maguindanao, the largest group, are concentrated mostly in the Cotabato region of Mindanao. The Maranao live in the two Lanao provinces, mostly in the Lake Lanao region. Their close kin, the Iranun, or Illanun, inhabit the Lanao region around Illana Bay and the northern Cotabato region. The Tausug and Samal live in the Sulu Archipelago, whereas others of them have settled on Basilan Island and in Zamboanga del Sur. The Jama Mapun live on the island of Cagayan de Sulu; the Yakan, on Basilan. The Sangil live in Davao as well as on the Sarangani Islands and parts of Cotabato. The Kalagan live along the shores of the Davao Gulf. The Kolibugan are concentrated mostly in Zamboanga del Sur. The Palawani live in southern Palawan Island; the Molbog, or Melebuganon, on nearby Balabac Island, which is just off the northern coast of Borneo.

Many of the Muslim dialects share similarities: both the Maguindanao and Maranao languages, for example, can be spoken and understood by both groups. But some languages and dialects spoken by Muslims are more akin to Christian ones: the closely related Samal, Jama Mapun, and Badjao are yet quite different from Tausug, which resembles the Tagalog and Visayan spoken mostly by Christians. Nonetheless, the various languages and dialects of Christian and Muslim Filipinos are all derived from the same linguistic family, according to modern linguists, and share many similarities. After all, both Muslim and Christian Filipinos belong to the Malay race.

The Muslim groups also differ in their occupations. The Maguindanao are an agricultural people who cultivate wet rice. The Maranao cultivate upland rice and corn; they are also famous for their brasswork and weaving. Spirited traders, they can be found selling their wares almost anyplace in the Philippines. Most of the Iranun are farmers, but some are fishermen. Those Tausug who live inland on Jolo Island are farmers, whereas the coastal Tausug and Samal are fishermen and barter traders. The Yakan of Basilan Island cultivate upland rice and root crops but rarely fish, whereas the Samal living on the island's coast are fishermen. The Kalagan are both traders and fishermen. Tagalog Muslims, on the other hand, are highly urbanized: some are professionals, some office workers, some factory workers. Factory workers are rare, however, in the predominantly Muslim areas because there is little, if any, manufacturing or similar industry.

The Muslim groups differ markedly in the practice of their cultural traditions and customary laws (*adat*), some of which were established before the advent of Islam. In general, however, the groups share a similar social structure. Throughout their history, this social, as well as political, structure has been based on the *datu* system, which was also, like the *adat*, a pre-Islamic institution. The *datu* was a local or petty ruler, or princeling, with executive and military powers. One might inherit such status or acquire it through military prowess, wealth, or astuteness. With the advent of Islam, a few powerful *datus* eventually assumed the title of sultan; but there was always tension between sultans and less powerful *datus*. To solidify their power and establish their rule as ostensibly legitimate, sultans claimed descent from the Prophet Muhammad. Today there are still *datus* among Muslim Filipinos, although many of their former powers have been diminished.

In past centuries, single Muslim groups constituted independent political units, or some combined to form political aggregations. Sometimes there was fighting, as well as economic rivalry, among them. But when in common danger from external threats, they usually cooperated in military defense. There was also frequent intermarriage between their ruling families, for economic and political purposes. Today, however, intermarriage between the groups is increasing among the other social classes as well because modern technology has made transportation and communication easier and has greatly reduced the relative isolation of the groups. Previously, Manila, as the educational center and capital of the country, was often the sole source of contact between members of the different groups.

There are also differences among the Muslim groups in their applied forms of Islamic practices and institutions. Groups who were exposed to Islam earlier in history tend to believe that their forms of practice are thus more sophisticated or more orthodox than those of other groups. Perhaps as a reflection of this, adherence to traditional practices and rituals of Islam is more evident in the larger towns than in the rural areas. And as a result of the earlier Islamic influence on the groups that settled near large population centers, their established *adat* changed sooner, becoming less pervasive in their daily lives, whereas the *adat* of more rural groups were preserved longer: the degree of influence of the *adat* varies among the groups even today.

But, regardless of their differences, Muslims in the Philippines all consider themselves Muslims and identify with each other. They are constantly aware that their religion is distinct from the religions of other Filipinos. They are not fazed by remarks some foreign Muslim visitors make that particular practices among them are not truly Islamic. Nonetheless, their religious leaders—especially those who have studied abroad in Arab countries—continually instruct the faithful to adhere to other practices that these leaders have learned as more orthodox or truer to Islam.

All Muslim Filipinos recognize each other as members of a wider religious community that transcends linguistic, racial, tribal, and national boundaries. They all pray together, within or outside their communities. Regardless of the degree of their participation in national or civic affairs, or in other institutions and associations, the major source of their identity is Islam. It is an identity that has been shaped by historical forces of the last four or five centuries and that has been endangered but reinforced by the dramatic events, the tragic turmoil and fighting, of the last two or three decades.

tian Filipinos and Muslim Filipinos. Spanish military expeditions devastated Muslim communities and farms and destroyed thousands of seacraft, disrupting the lives and economy of an agricultural, fishing, and commercial people. During many of the expeditions, larger Muslim towns were deliberately depopulated: the inhabitants were destroyed or enslaved. Similarly, Muslim raids on Spanish coastal settlements were so devastating (thousands of Christianized natives were carried off for sale in the slave markets) that the name *moro* came to acquire the connotation of a barbarous pirate and slave trader.

The motivating force behind these wars was religious difference. The Spanish colonial government and ecclesiastical authorities indoctrinated the Christianized natives with the belief that Muslims were inveterate enemies of their new religion. *Te Deum* masses were held following major Spanish victories. During the celebration of a Spanish victory in 1637, Spanish Jesuits presented a morality play, which became the model for all the so-called *moro-moro* plays. Defeat of the Muslims was always enacted in these plays, and the drama often concluded with the conversion of a Muslim chief, or his daughter falling in love with a brave and handsome Spanish officer. Spaniards were portrayed as noble gentlemen exemplifying Christian virtues, whereas the Moros were portrayed as ugly, slovenly, treacherous, untrustworthy, and fanatical. All major towns eventually included such plays in the festivities honoring their patron saints. *Moro-moro* plays became part of the cultural activities of the towns and served as tools of propaganda by promoting a negative image of the Moros and of all Muslims. Even after the decline of the Spanish regime and up to the eve of the Japanese-American War, these plays were still being performed in Philippine provinces. Many of the older generation of Filipinos can vividly remember them; probably the attitudes of many Filipinos toward Moros today have been shaped or influenced by exposure to them during childhood.

The Muslim counterparts of the Spanish priests were preachers who condemned the Spaniards and their Christianized native subordinates as enemies of Islam and as doomed to

CHAPTER TWO

WESTERN IMPERIALISM

*   *   *

THE GEOGRAPHICAL LOCATION of the Philippines caused it to be drawn gradually into the international maritime trade that extended from the Red Sea to the China Sea. From the ninth century C.E. to the early sixteenth century, this trade was controlled almost wholly by Muslim merchants. Muslim traders are known to have visited Borneo in the tenth century, and some settled in Sulu as early as the thirteenth century. By this time, Muslim traders were often stopping at islands in the Philippines on their way north to China. In the next century, Muslim preachers (*makhdumin*) from nearby Indonesian islands arrived in Sulu on a missionary endeavor. These *makhdumin*, some undoubtedly influenced by Sufism, taught the basic elements of Islam and erected simple mosques.

In the last decade of the fourteenth century, when the vestiges of the Kingdom of Srivijaya were being swept away by Majapahit, there was an exodus of many Sumatran princes and warriors to different parts of the Malay world. Sulu *tarsilas* (Ar. *silsila*)[1] tell of a Sumatran prince with ministers and followers who landed at Buansa on Jolo Island to found a principality. They were confronted by native Muslims, and fighting broke out. The accounts are vague about a probable victory for the *baguinda*: they tell only that the local chiefs welcomed him when he identified himself and his followers as Muslims. The *baguinda* became a local rajah and married a native Muslim lady. According to Sulu legend, years later an Arab journeyed from Sumatra and Borneo to Buansa. He married a daughter of the *baguinda* and established a sultanate in about 1450, according to historians. All Sulu sultans have claimed descent from this first sultan.

When Malacca was at the height of its glory and had even become an Islamic theological center, many of its Muslim preachers migrated to other Malay lands to spread the faith. In 1511, however, this fabled Muslim international emporium fell to the Portuguese. Members of its royal family fled to other areas as refugees. Some founded new principalities, probably including a principality along the western shore of Mindanao. Its founders and their successors began to extend their power southward to what is now the province of Cotabato.

The fall of Malacca set the stage for Brunei to emerge as a leading Malay naval and commercial power. By the 1520s, an increasing number of Muslim Bornean traders and preachers were arriving in the Philippines. Also by this time, Manila had become a Muslim principality under a *datu*, or *rajah*, who was a kinsman of the Brunei sultan.

---

[1] *Tarsilas:* written genealogical accounts. Some include mythological elements, whereas others refer to authentic historical incidents. They normally deal with early settlers, movements of populations, sultans, and religious personalities.

* * *

THE COMING OF the Spaniards to the Philippines in 1565 establish a colony and to convert its inhabitants to Christianity is important in that it blocked any further spreading of Islam north from Borneo and the southern Philippines toward Luzon and the Visayan Islands. From then on, Islam would be confined to the Sulu Archipelago and western Mindanao.

By force, persuasion, or inducing submission with gifts the Spaniards were able to extend their sovereignty throughout the widely scattered Philippine settlements (*barangays*). But they met with fierce resistance from at least three sultanates in the South—those of Sulu, Maguindanao, and Buayan —which were political entities that had developed far beyond the simple structure of the *barangay*. The Spaniards spared no efforts in men and resources to colonize and to convert the Muslims; their hatred for Islam and its institutions intensified with every failed effort. The Spaniards compelled natives whom they had converted, to serve as their allies in combat these natives served as rowers, spearmen, or warriors in attacks against Muslim settlements and forts. They were indoctrinated with the belief that they were performing a religious service. The Christian *indio*, then, was pitted against the recalcitrant *moro*.[2] Thus the Crusades of medieval Europe were extended to Malay lands.

The long series of wars between the Spaniards and the Muslims have been called the "Moro Wars," and they continued up to the twilight of Spanish rule in the Philippines. Their effects cannot be overemphasized: they contributed to the tensions and conflicts that exist today between Christ

---

[2] *Moro:* When the Spaniards came to the Philippines in the second half of the sixteenth century, they used the term *moro* to refer to inhabitants professing Islam. *Indio* gradually came to denote natives who became Christians. Unconverted pagans in the mountains or interior of large islands were called *infieles*. By the seventeenth century, these terms were rarely confused in Spanish accounts. The term *Filipino* was, almost up to the last years of the Spanish colonial regime, normally reserved for Spaniards born in the Philippines to distinguish them from the *peninsulares*, who were Spaniards born in Spain.

eternal perdition. Spaniards were ridiculed as licentious pork eaters and greedy marauders who had come to take what they lacked in their own country. Christian natives were ridiculed as servants, mere puppets who were being used by the Spaniards for their imperialistic purposes. This "betrayal" by the native Filipinos would always be deeply resented by the Muslims, for they had once recognized that the two groups shared a common ancestry.

The Moro Wars and the Spanish strategy of "divide and conquer" during them have left a legacy of bitter attitudes not easily canceled in a few generations. Bitterness still persists in some segments of the Philippine population. But it is notably absent among the youth, especially university students. In spite of attempts by some romanticists to revive the *moro-moro* plays as part of the Filipino cultural heritage, they have not been performed in at least the last thirty years.

Another result of the Moro Wars was the strengthening of certain Islamic and *adat* institutions. When help from neighboring Muslim principalities outside the Philippines was cut off because they had fallen to European powers, Muslim sultanates in the Philippines were forced to develop their own resources. During the wars the sultanate governments became more centralized for purposes of defense. The power of the local *'ulama* (the religious leadership) increased. Before battle they could be seen exhorting the faithful to victory. Loyalty to the chiefs and defense of family, home, and ancestral lands became Islamic duties. Muslims killed in battle were considered martyrs. Islam helped to unite the sultanates and to provide them with a sense of "nationalism." It served as the major source of identity for Muslims fighting the Spaniards and their native allies.

In the last quarter of the nineteenth century, Spanish official policy no longer focused on converting the Muslims; instead, it aimed at merely transforming them into peaceable and submissive subjects of the Spanish monarchy. But Spanish missionaries continued trying to convince the colonial government that the Moros would become better subjects only if they became Christians first. Meanwhile, Spanish military expeditions into Muslim territories were, at last, winning victories. The long and frequent wars had devastated Muslim lands and had weakened their economy and military power. And so Spanish military power—especially their navy—surpassed that of the Muslims. Some sultans were forced to enter into peace treaties with the colonial government in Manila, and many *datus* volunteered to submit to and to accept Spanish protection. Nonetheless, most Muslim chiefs did not care for the subtle details and possible pitfalls in treaty stipulations. They never really believed that they were conquered and were only biding their time for circumstances that would allow them to regain their independence.

This was the situation the Americans found when they came to wrest control of the Philippines from Spain in 1898. Later the Filipino revolutionary government under Emilio Aguinaldo and the subsequent government of the First Philippine Republic would try to enlist the aid of Muslims in defending the country against the Americans. These efforts would fail, however, mainly because the Muslim sultans and *datus* distrusted Christian Filipinos, whom they had fought in the past. The traditional Muslim leaders judged these new Filipino governments to be just as Christian—and so just as inimical—as that of the Spanish colonial régime.

* * *

WHEN THE AMERICANS came to Muslim lands after their arrival in the Philippines, they initially labeled the inhabitants savages who needed to be pacified. Then they began to view the Muslims as similar to the American Indians. Some of their best Indian warriors were sent to fight the Muslims. Resistance against them was launched by various *datus* acting on their own initiative. Often, individual families took it upon themselves to fight American troops. But because certain influential sultans and *datus* were given gifts, salaries, and flatteries, there was no united action against the Americans. And because of the Americans' superiority in weapons —including their use of dumdum bullets and the newly introduced .45 caliber pistol—they were able to gain sovereignty over the Muslim groups and to incorporate them into the

American colony of the Philippines. The Americans then assumed responsibility for westernizing the Muslims so they would be as capable of governing themselves as the Christian Filipinos, at least at certain administrative levels. They sent Christian Filipino civil officials to Muslim areas to introduce new ways of government to the Muslims and to encourage both communities to cooperate in civic projects, in hopes of reducing deep-rooted Christian-Muslim animosity. Possibly, as part of this program, they encouraged Christian Filipinos to settle in Mindanao. Before World War I, they were even responsible for establishing at least seven agricultural colonies in traditional Muslim areas. Unlike the Spaniards, the Americans did not encourage Christian-Muslim animosity. By sending thousands of Christian settlers to Muslim lands, however, they sowed seeds of tensions and conflict between the two communities.

It was official American policy to leave untouched the Muslims' religious life and their practice of Islamic rituals. Nonetheless, Islam was alien and strange to most American officials—something to be feared or despised. They looked with suspicion and disfavor on visits by foreign, especially Arab, Muslims to the Muslim South. They discouraged contacts between Muslims in the Philippines and their brothers on the neighboring island of Borneo or on other Indonesian islands. It was even the view among some military officers and government administrators, including Leonard Wood and John Pershing, that inhibiting their Islamic life would cause the Muslims to fraternize with Christian and other Filipinos, and they would therefore be more easily pacified and governed. This view indeed echoed that of the Jesuits during the last years of Spanish rule.

In spite of their lack of respect for the traditional *datu* system, American officials never made a real effort to abolish it. They suppressed certain recalcitrant *datus* but maintained friendly relations with—indeed, even pampered—those who had readily accepted American sovereignty. Thus, continuance of the system was ensured. But as an ironic result, the novel political institutions and techniques the Americans had introduced in Christian areas were not nurtured in Muslim areas. Since the Christian Filipinos were already to some extent influenced by Western ideas brought by Spanish colonization, American administrators found it easier to communicate and deal with them. Also, Christian Filipinos began to cooperate with the administration and so gained choice positions in the government. Contrariwise, Muslims generally did not show such enthusiasm to participate in the new system. Thus, the Americans' plan to groom the Muslims for independence was altered and tailored to the Christian Filipinos. This happened in 1920 when the Muslim provinces fell to the governance of Christian Filipinos who were eager to inherit the imperial mantle on the date of independence as promised by the United States.

Except for a few, Muslim leaders generally shied away from the nationalist movement for an independent Philippine nation. Many who had previously fought the Americans now decided to opt for government under an American protectorate as a better alternative to subjugation to Christian Filipinos. This was the gist of a petition that Sulu *datus* and leaders submitted to government authorities in 1921. A similar petition was drawn up in the next three years and was eventually received by the United States Congress. In March 1935, more than one hundred Maranao *datus* wrote to President Roosevelt expressing the desire to be excluded from the proposed independent Philippine state. Instead, they wanted to be under the protection and tutelage of the United States until they would be able to form their own independent state. They maintained that in an independent Philippine nation Muslims would not be allowed to participate in administration nor to share in economic gains. Moreover, they were not at all confident that Islam would be respected or even acknowledged by a Filipino government.

Some Americans supported the Muslim petitions, because they felt either spite toward Filipino nationalists or genuine sympathy with the Muslims' cause. Also, there was a pressure group with American economic interests who wanted Mindanao and Sulu to be made into a separate political entity —independent of the rest of the country—and governed by a special commission. This plan emerged as the Bacon Bill and was presented to the United States Congress in 1926. This bill became an issue that served to unite Filipino nationalists against what they charged was a sinister American scheme to divide the country and to cater to American economic interests. The Bacon Bill died in Congress, however.

CHAPTER THREE

A SEPARATE PEOPLE
IN A NEW NATION
* * *

THE PHILIPPINE COMMONWEALTH government was established in 1935. The nation's new leaders in Manila had assumed that with self-government followed by full independence in the next decade, all segments of the population would cooperate and unite behind the national leadership, thrusting aside their conflicts and differences. But these leaders failed to understand the spirit of the Muslims and the nature of their aspirations and proved insensitive to their economic problems. Presuming that their own more sophisticated way of life was superior to that of the Muslims, these new government leaders believed that, with better education and a large dose of cultural indoctrination, the Muslims would eventually conform to the westernized ways of the new government and the Christian majority. Spanish and American colonial preconceptions—that the Muslims and other native minority groups could be westernized—had obviously influenced the new government's manner of thinking.

When Manuel Quezon, the president of the Commonwealth, declared that there would be no place for sultans and *datus* in the new regime and that the national laws would apply to Muslims and Christians equally, he was surprised at the Muslims' reactions. Apparently, he was unaware that the Muslims had their own cherished code of ethics and system of laws that governed virtually every aspect of their lives. He failed to realize that the national laws, which were enacted without representation of the Muslim constituency, upheld standards drawn from Christian ethics and Western social history. These laws were therefore alien to the Muslim Filipinos, whose cultural heritage was drawn largely from ancient Malay societies. Quezon's flagrant disregard for the traditional Muslim social and legal systems provoked resentment among Muslim leaders. The communities shared the resentment of their leaders, since the long wars had infused them all, leaders and followers, with common sentiments and a common purpose of self-preservation.

The Muslims also resented the new educational system, which emphasized Western "progressive" ideas that served to create a conformed new national citizenry. Rules of conduct were based on Western values. History books taught that the Muslims in the South, who had fought the Spaniards, were pirates and slave traders. Animals abhorred by Muslims appeared as characters in children's storybooks and as illustrations in their textbook exercises. Muslims were therefore not enthusiastic about their children attending public schools.

These are the reasons why Muslim religious leaders came to believe that the new government's legal and educational systems constituted an intentional scheme to extinguish Islam in the Philippines. And they are the reasons why Muslims refused to enter the mainstream of Philippine society.

*   *   *

TO DECREASE LAND disputes in the central provinces of Luzon, to reduce the population in the congested areas of some provinces, to increase agricultural productivity, and to discourage Japanese colonial ambitions in the South, the Commonwealth government launched a program to send thousands of Christian settlers to Mindanao, the "land of promise." Certain conditions were specified: the Christians were to settle in thinly populated areas only, and they were to respect the rights of native Muslim inhabitants.

There were also thousands of settlers from the North, who were not sponsored by the government but came on their own initiative. At least 10 thousand settlers came to occupy the Koronadal Valley in Cotabato; others settled elsewhere in the Cotabato and Lanao provinces. Many of them were poor and ignorant. The Muslims often helped them in the beginning, sharing their own work animals, their crude tools and equipment. *Datus* generally welcomed the settlers; some even "adopted" them. The government began to improve the old roads while building new ones to accommodate the influx of settlers. The government simplified the application process for land ownership titles to make it easier for new settlers to acquire land. All this puzzled the Muslims, for at first they did not realize that their very way of life was now threatened, that they were indeed being robbed of the ancestral lands so precious to them. Few could anticipate the economic and political ramifications of this Christian migration from Luzon and the Visayas to the Muslim South. Few could anticipate the struggle and bloodshed this migration would cause in the next two or three decades.

The Commonwealth government made modest efforts to incorporate some Muslim leaders into its administrative structure. It made modest efforts to raise the economic level and to improve social conditions for all Filipinos—including Muslims—but it had no well-defined program, and it had no conception of the strong Muslim heritage, nor any sensitivity to their particular conditions. The nation's leaders were more concerned with the immediate problems of land disputes in

the central provinces and of Japanese ambitions for control
of the entire country. The government was preoccupied
with party politics and its own internal power struggles. Any
development projects introduced in Mindanao were meant
to benefit the Christian settlers. The highest government positions in Mindanao and Sulu were not held by Muslims. It
was becoming difficult for Muslims to support a central government from which they received so little aid. Even the intellectuals, the prominent and sophisticated members of Muslim
communities, considered themselves victims of discrimination
—a minority class of inferior status in a country where their
voice could not be heard.

＊　＊　＊

IN THE EARLY months of 1942, Japanese troops invaded
Muslim territories in the Philippines. The occupation troops
treated the Muslims as harshly as they did other Filipinos.
Thousands of Muslims joined guerrilla units and cooperated
with Christians in harassing the Japanese. A dozen or more
prominent *datus* tolerated Japanese policies in order to allay
severe Japanese retaliation against Muslim communities. Yet
apparently none of these leaders ever took a strong public
stand against the United States. Some guerrilla chiefs working
closely with Americans against the Japanese were even kinsmen of these *datus*.

The fall of the Commonwealth government to the Japanese
inspired many *datus* and other leaders to act independently
of a central government, for many Muslim communities chose
to remain self-contained and isolated. Outlaw bands and Muslim farmers tried to provoke Christian settlers to leave, and
many settlers did migrate to the towns.

Japanese occupation had important effects on postwar relations between the Muslims, on the one hand, and the government and Christians, on the other. The resistance against
the Japanese had revealed that there were times when Muslims and Christians could cooperate. After the defeat of the
Japanese, the Commonwealth government appointed eminent
Muslim guerrilla leaders to high administrative positions in

provinces where Muslims formed a majority. This practice was continued by the succeeding government of the Republic. The major national parties began to induce Muslim leaders to join their ranks, so these leaders were exposed to a milieu different from that of their constituencies.

Another effect was the wide distribution of arms and ammunition among both Muslims and Christians in Sulu and Mindanao. During the war, American submarines regularly brought arms from Australia and distributed them among guerrilla units in Mindanao. Sometimes these arms were given to Muslim units, which were then once again transformed into armed bands under strong leaders. Government efforts to retrieve these arms later were never fully successful.

Back pay to guerrillas and reparation payments to families who filed claims for destroyed properties helped fund the construction of new mosques and Qur'anic schools *(madrasas)*. Financial contributions to help fund religious festivities were numerous and often impressive, because a donor always gained prestige in his community. Most important, the suddenly increased money supply for many years enabled hundreds of Muslim families to go on the *hajj* (pilgrimage to Mecca). A returned *haji* always gained a high status in his community. The time would come when the yearly number of pilgrims would surpass one thousand, regardless of the sources or amount of funding.

All the above promoted a resurgence of Islam. Moreover, the suddenly increased money supply allowed Muslims to buy and trade goods and commodities they had never known in their barter system of economy. They began to aspire to salaried jobs and professional careers and a higher status in the business world. "These two factors—resurgent Islam and the shifting basis of the Moro economy from barter to cash— helped to fuel post–World War II Moro dissatisfaction with their place in the Philippine Republic."[3]

---

[3] Peter G. Gowing, *Muslim Filipinos—Heritage and Horizon* (Quezon City: New Day Publishers, 1979), p. 183.

＊　＊　＊

THE PHILIPPINES WERE declared an independent republic on July 4, 1946. Many Muslims found both local and national positions in the new administration. They ran for election to political offices as members of either of the two major political parties, and many were successful. Although they indulged in the usual politicking, Muslim politicians generally tried to gain benefits for their constituencies. Yet they had been absorbed into a system that had given them opportunities for advancement and to which they were indebted; and with greater exposure to national problems, these Muslim leaders developed an affinity with the national political body. But most Muslims did not share this sense of national identity, for many reasons.

First, Muslims found it difficult to appreciate the national laws, especially those pertaining to personal or family relations, for they were clearly derived from Western or Catholic moral values. Muslims could not understand why national law did not provide for polygyny and divorce, which Islamic Holy Law allowed the faithful. Because they could not accept the premise that the laws and moral values of other peoples were superior to theirs, Muslims continued to structure their family life according to their tradition—often in violation of national laws. It was clear that Muslims and Christians in the Philippines represented two different cultures with many points of conflict. Because of pressure from Muslim politicians, who were in turn under pressure from fellow Muslims, the government occasionally enacted temporary laws recognizing the Muslim form of marriages—but always with the assumption that marriages between Muslims would eventually come to be governed by civil law rather than by the *shari'a*. In matters of inheritance, Muslims were inclined to follow their *adat*.

Second, the public school system under the Republic did not differ much from that which the Americans had introduced and the Commonwealth had developed. Even if the government had tried, it would have found it difficult to convince Muslim parents that the school system was not meant to alienate their children from Islam. But unfortunately, the government did not try to convince Muslims otherwise. Instead, it implemented the same curriculum for Filipino children in all regions regardless of religious or cultural differences. Because its purpose was to weld all segments of the population into a national community and to foster nationalism, the government would see to it that all students were educated in one definite direction. Worthy and understandable as this purpose was, the government nonetheless had failed to consider that the Muslims had certain unique religious characteristics and their own separate history, which they wanted their children to learn about. Muslims naturally became apprehensive when Christian schools were established in their midst, for it was apparent that these were operated by missionaries. Needless to say, Muslim suspicions about non-Islamic schools stemmed from their past experiences with institutions the Spanish colonial government had imposed on them.

Further, the educational problems of the Muslims were compounded by specific difficulties that their religious schools (*madrasas*) suffered. There was a chronic lack of textbooks, competent faculty, and facilities. Moreover, although these schools performed their religious function, they did not provide Muslim students with knowledge about their region and country or foster in them determination to seek ways to improve the socioeconomic conditions of their communities.

* * *

A THIRD REASON for Muslims' inability to consider themselves citizens of the Republic was their deep resentment of—and later, violent reaction to—the steady influx of settlers to parts of Mindanao. More than 200 thousand Christians had come to the Cotabato region in the past forty years, reducing what was once a Muslim majority to a minority of 30 percent. In many of their traditional areas, the Muslim population had all but disappeared by the 1960s. A similar population shift took place in the northern Lanao area. For example, in 1918, there were only about 24 Christian families living in the Kapatagan

Basin, which is in the western part of what is now the province of Lanao del Norte. In 1941, there were 8 thousand Christians in that area, and in 1960, 93 thousand Christians, many of whom had come there under the sponsorship of a government development plan. In contrast, only about 7 thousand Maranao Muslims remained there in 1960.[4]

During the administration of President Ramon Magsaysay (1953–1957), thousands of pardoned criminals and ex-Communists who had surrendered to the government were granted homesteads. Agricultural colonies were established in the midst of Muslim communal farms. The government facilitated the issuance of land titles to the Christian settlers it sponsored as well as to anyone literate enough to apply for them. But most Muslims were too illiterate to apply. Those few educated Muslims who acquired titles acquired lands that formerly had been communal. In land disputes between settlers who had titles and Muslims who had none, the settlers had little difficulty persuading the authorities to evict the Muslims from their land. Whenever Muslims received some compensation from the settlers, however, and as long as land was still available somewhere, tensions were eased. Sometimes Muslims would accept payment for the land they tilled, and then their relatives would demand additional payment from the buyer. Because their idea of land distribution was based on communal rather than on title ownership, and because they wanted to take advantage of the situation, these

[4]Before the declaration of Philippine independence in 1946, Cotabato, Lanao, and Sulu each were single whole provinces. To satisfy political bosses as well as for demographic purposes, the government later subdivided these three provinces: Cotabato was divided into North Cotabato, South Cotabato, Sultan Kudarat, and Maguindanao. Lanao was divided into Lanao del Norte and Lanao del Sur. Tawi-Tawi is now separate from Sulu.

In 1918 there were 110,926 Muslims and 61,052 non-Muslims in Cotabato Province. By 1970 the Muslim population had grown to 424,577, whereas that of non-Muslims, including the transplanted settlers, was 711,430 in this province. In 1918 there were 83,319 Muslims and 8,140 non-Muslims in Lanao Province. By 1970, the total number of Muslims was 497,122 (416,269 in Lanao del Sur and 80,853 in Lanao del Norte), and that of non-Muslims was 308,328 (39,239 in Lanao del Sur and 269,089 in Lanao del Norte). The population of Sulu is overwhelmingly Muslim. There has never been a settler problem in Sulu: an alleged plan to send settlers to Tawi-Tawi did not materialize because of the disturbances there in the last decade or so.

Muslims believed what they were doing was right. Often they even resorted to intimidation or force.

By the 1950s, there were so many Christian settlers that they controlled entire towns and were equipped to protect them. Then additional settlers came from other islands to live in the towns and engage in trade. A time would come when there would be both landless Muslims and landless Christians in Cotabato, and disputes would become more frequent.

The increase of the non-Muslim population in Cotabato and parts of Lanao led many Muslims to conclude that there was a deliberate government scheme either to disperse them or to ensure that they remain a permanent minority in their own territories. They noted with frustration, if not envy, that the areas where the Christians had settled now had better roads and more effective irrigation projects, civic centers, and schools in comparison with their own backward facilities. So they believed that they were the victims of government discrimination and of neglect by their own leaders. In turn, Muslim leaders blamed all the ills on the so-called Christian government in Manila.

*   *   *

ALTHOUGH THERE WAS no Muslim revolt or even any organized threat against the new Republic in the early 1950s, there was an increase of tensions and a breakdown of law and order in some Muslim areas. In Sulu this was mainly a result of poverty and unemployment. Outlaw bands sprang up throughout the South. In 1954, the Philippine Senate created a committee to study and make recommendations on the "Moro Problem." Headed by a prominent Muslim leader, Domocao Alonto Haji Ahmad, the committee brought out the land disputes and stated that the Muslims in the country did not feel as if they belonged to the nation. It made various recommendations, but apparently only one was fully carried out: the creation of the Commission on National Integration. Its purpose was to accelerate the progress of Muslims politically, economically, and socially and to promote their incorporation into the nation's government and social systems.

Instead, the Commission concentrated on granting scholarships to Muslims and other cultural minority groups. Before it was combined with other agencies in 1975, it succeeded in providing thousands of Muslims with higher education at academic institutions in Manila—although not as many as desired or anticipated actually succeeded in completing degrees. It can be assumed that the voicing in recent years of Muslim aspirations and expectations has been made by those Muslims who have become politically conscious of the conditions in their communities as a result of their education through government sponsorship. This ironically implies the success—partial, at least—of government scholarships. After a while, however, *datus* and other more affluent Muslims began to finance their sons' education with their own resources if scholarships were unavailable. It was the rise of a Muslim professional class—mostly lawyers—in the mid-1950s and early 1960s, that led to a voicing of Muslim aspirations. In the late 1960s and early 1970s, this group was reinforced with hundreds of Muslim university students who promoted social and political reform. A few Muslim student organizations were formed. Although cliquish, with leaders who set their eyes toward future political roles, these organizations made conscious efforts to set aside ethnic and linguistic differences, a goal that could be attained only by emphasizing a common Islamic identity.

But the qualitative change in Muslims' awareness of themselves as a people and in their knowledge of Islam was fostered by thousands of young Muslims who studied abroad in Islamic institutions under foreign scholarships. At times during the 1950s and 1960s more than a hundred students each year were studying in Al-Azhar University in Cairo. Others were enrolled in professional schools and even in a military academy. Upon their return, they began to correct local practices that they believed contradicted religious law and, in their own way, tried to abolish superstitions that many of the older generation believed constituted part of the faith. Many of these Muslims educated abroad began to teach in *madrasas*; others worked for Muslim politicians and the traditional leaders. Thus, in effect, many of them would form the core of a new *'ulama'*. Along with the Muslim professionals and university students, they, too, embodied an important and prestigious means for voicing Muslim aspirations for the socioeconomic and cultural development of their communities.

But the emergence of a new *'ulama*—which is one of the most important characteristics of the postwar Islamic revivalist movement in the Philippines—would not have been possible without the gaining of independence of more than a score of Muslim nations. These were principally Arab and were themselves experiencing an increased consciousness of Islam. After World War II, foreign Muslims who had come to observe the religious and social situation of Muslims in the Philippines to determine their needs returned to their home countries and urged their Muslim associations to send religious teachers to the Philippines. And when Muslim Filipino politicians and professionals traveled abroad and visited Muslim countries, they were given overwhelming welcomes and were showered with questions. This treatment in itself began to awaken within the Filipino visitors a latent consciousness of Islam and of their social duty to the community. Contacts made during their travels often resulted in offers of scholarships, teachers, and religious literature. Invitations to international Muslim conferences inevitably followed. Muslims in other parts of the world became aware of the plight of their Muslim brothers in the Philippines and expressed concern. Hundreds of scholarships were offered to Muslim Filipino politicians, who then chose candidates for them. It was these politicians who, in their efforts to repair the *madrasa* system, first requested that Muslim institutions abroad send religious teachers to the Philippines. These foreign teachers were also to serve as *imams* in mosques built by funds these politicians were able to raise. Of course the politicians did not let their constituencies forget their role in securing such benefits. Their constituents were thus indebted to them, and so the ancient *datu* tradition—the bond between *datus* and their followers—was further reinforced.

Various local, regional, and national Muslim organizations were founded during this period. These organizations often indulged in rivalry and petty squabbling with each other.

And since the problems of the Muslims were political, economic, and social as well as religious, organizations served as political bases for their leaders. But in its own style each helped expand awareness of Islam and revive it within the communities.

Clearly, Muslim leadership in the country was fragmented. By 1970, when confrontation between Muslims and government armed forces and Christian armed bands was imminent, it had become imperative for all leaders and their organizations to unite in common action. But this was more complicated than it would appear. A Muslim government religious official from another country might come to the Philippines to arrange a merger of leadership, only to bungle all efforts toward mediation by helping form yet another organization. So even foreign Muslim countries often promoted their own favorites for the official head of a Muslim movement in the Philippines.

* * *

AT THIS POINT we might summarize the several interrelated factors that awakened in Filipinos an increased Muslim consciousness of Islam and of themselves as a people comprising a religious community that was separate from the rest of the Philippine population. These factors include the rise of a new *'ulama*, whose numbers swelled with hundreds of graduates from Islamic institutions abroad, and the rise of a professional group. There was also a dramatic increase of Muslim Filipino university students in general, and an increase of returning *hajis*—an average of at least one thousand a year. There was the importation of teachers from abroad, mostly Egyptian religious scholars, who came to teach Arabic and Islam in the *madrasas* or to serve in mosques. There were the visits from foreign Muslim officials and scholars, the invitation of local Muslim leaders and scholars to international Muslim conferences abroad, and the donation of Islamic religious literature by foreign Muslims. Finally, there was the example set by religious movements in other Muslim countries.

Further, along with the above factors that directly stimu-
lated Muslims' consciousness of Islam was the formation of
many organizations that either were Islamic in nature or were
restricted to an exclusively Muslim membership. Many new
madrasas were built, and every Muslim population center had
erected its own mosque. The recaptured concept that Muslims
in the Philippines composed an *umma* that was not only separate from the rest of the country but also really part of a wider
umma that transcended national boundaries became firmly
rooted. Ironically, this sense of identity was reinforced as a
result of the great influx of settlers from other islands, which
had reduced the Muslims to a minority in areas where they
had once been a majority. This gradual depopulation of Muslims was especially painful for the traditional leaders, whose
ancestors had once ruled such areas. In the late 1950s, when
the process of electing local officials was extended to Mindanao, Christian candidates invariably won because formerly
Muslim towns were now inhabited by a Christian majority.
The Muslim candidates who lost were, of course, bitter. Some
of those who had initially welcomed—indeed, had even helped
—new settlers began to warn their followers of the danger in
losing the ancestral lands to the newcomers. Because the Muslims were becoming aware of their history of resistance to out-
siders, of themselves as a religious people different from the
newcomers, and of the need to live close together as a group
in order to maintain their Islamic institutions, the preservation of their lands and integrity of their religious community
became intimate, sometimes overlapping, political issues for
the traditional leaders. So Muslim candidates mistakenly believed they would have to contend with only their Christian
opponents, and that all Muslims, regardless of different social
origins or economic status, would unite politically. But instead,
rivalry developed among these traditional leaders and weakened
their stand against the Christian candidates.

By the 1960s—in spite of a fragmented leadership, rivalry
among Muslim politicians on the national and local levels,
ethnolinguistic differences, and the absorption of some Muslim leaders into the national structure—it was clear what the
Muslim Filipinos wanted for themselves as a religious com-

munity and as part of a larger political body. They were a
people trying to preserve and enhance their religion and culture despite such obstacles as national laws that conflicted
with their Holy Law and a national educational system that
conflicted with their religious principles and ethnic identity.
They were a people who had suddenly become aware that
their social and economic conditions were backward relative
to those of the Christians, and who thus desired immediate
improvement of their conditions. They were a people with
a strong sense of their history who desired to regain the territory they and their leaders had once held as their domain.
Moreover, their leaders desired greater involvement in the
national political process and in decisions affecting the destiny of their people.

The Muslims' aspirations, demands, and expectations were
certain to cause disturbances in some localities. The government viewed these disturbances as problems of law and order,
which required police or military intervention. The government's former policy of assimilation—efforts to make the
Muslims think and act like "the others"—had obviously failed.
Its subsequent policy—that of incorporating them into the
national system so that they would think of themselves as Filipinos—was not working either, since naturally they would
not feel any loyalty to a nation that discriminated against them
or did not offer them equal benefits. But because Muslims
were now being elected to national and local political offices
and were serving in government positions, the government
could not understand why disturbances were still flaring up.
The fact was that Muslims' holding of political offices often
boosted their own personal economic status but did not necessar-
ily lead to their improving the conditions in their communities.

Various Senate committee reports have emphasized that
the land problems in Cotabato were caused by the great influx
of settlers from other provinces and by the government's failure to help Muslims increase their productivity. For example,
a report revealed that, until 1971, there were no irrigation
projects in any areas with predominantly Muslim populations.
This was not the case in areas where the Christian settlers
were in the majority. These reports neglected to mention that,

in areas where Muslims had become a minority, no Muslim could be elected to a political office. There were land disputes or very poor conditions and neglected communities in other parts of the country as well. In the postwar period there was an armed Communist rebellion in the central provinces of Luzon. But the Muslims' attitude of resistance was always different from that of the other minority groups in the country: they always thought of the government as that of the majority—that is, of "the others."

CHAPTER FOUR

MASSACRES AND MOVEMENT
FOR INDEPENDENCE

* * *

IT WAS LOGICAL that Muslim politicians on both national and local levels would take up the cause of their people—for whatever motives, altruistic or otherwise. In 1961, Datu Ombra Amilbangsa, a congressman from Sulu, introduced a bill in Congress requesting the government to grant independence to the entire province of Sulu. He was one of the three pretenders to the Sulu sultanate and had been crowned a sultan by his followers some years before. The bill was publicized by the press and drew comments from historians and others interested in Muslim affairs; but nothing came of it in Congress, where it was considered a mere curiosity. Nonetheless, like many efforts of its kind, the bill generated expectations among the dissatisfied Tausugs and Samals. Although there was not the settler problem in Sulu that there was in Cotabato and Lanao, there were many landless farmers. Unemployment was high because the time-honored barter system of trade with Borneo had been eliminated and because of an increase in population. Bad roads, poor and inadequate schools, and sanitation problems compounded the difficulties. Sulu had the lowest literacy rate—that is, number of inhabitants who could read and write either English or the local dialect—in the country.

The incident that accelerated tensions between Muslims and the government, however, was the so-called Corregidor Incident, or Jabidah Massacre, of March 1968. Sometime in 1967, certain elements of the Philippine Army created a secret project called "Merdeka"—a mission to recruit and train young Muslims in Sulu, especially in the Samal areas, to form a special unit. At the end of the year, about 180 recruits were transferred to Corregidor Island, which is at the entrance to Manila Bay. The mission Merdeka was now called "Jabidah." The Muslim recruits were being trained in sabotage, jungle warfare, and guerrilla tactics, while vague reports of this covert activity filtered into some Muslim quarters but were either ignored or purposely dismissed.

Early one morning in March 1968, some Cavite fishermen returning home with their catch saw an exhausted man in the water clinging to a floating log. He had a bullet wound in one leg. He asked his rescuers to hide him, and then he revealed a tale so strange and startling that the fishermen took him to the governor of the province. The rescued man was Jibin Arula, one of the Muslim trainees in Corregidor. He told of how a general discontent among the trainees—and anger especially over a delay in their allowance—had sparked their demand that they be allowed to return to their homes. After an initial refusal, they were told they could go. They were brought to a tiny airstrip in groups of about twelve. Arula was in the third group, who were escorted to the airstrip at about four in the morning. Suddenly they were fired upon by regular army troops. Arula was only wounded, but four of his comrades were killed. He hid among the bushes, then managed to roll to the beach and swam toward Cavite, for he could see the distant lights. He clung to a floating log until his rescue four hours later.

The governor of Cavite, Justiniano Montano, gave Arula sanctuary. As a member of the political party opposing President Marcos, Montano allowed newspaper reporters to interview Arula and appeared to be enjoying his providential role of protector. Upon hearing of the incident, political opponents of the president raised a clamor against the administration and the army. The press took up the cry for justice. Congress and high military authorities routinely began forming their investigating committees. In time it was revealed that some of the top military authorities of the country were completely unaware of the existence of Jabidah. It was also revealed that there had been a mutiny among the Muslim trainees, after which possibly twenty-eight of them were executed without investigation or trial. A Christian army officer was also killed during the affair: there were rumors that he was one of the training directors and was shot for objecting to the treacherous executions of the trainees.

The congressional investigations were heavily publicized and even televised. The military officer in charge of Merdeka and Jabidah was identified as Major Eduardo Martelino, who had also adopted the name of Abdul Latif. He testified before Congress that Muslims had been recruited under the pretext that they would be trained as an armed unit for action in Sabah, but that the real purpose was ultimately to prevent them from engaging in any action there; Martelino neglected to explain exactly what they were meant to do once they were shaped into this armed unit. Under a barrage of questions, Martelino revealed so much that some officials expressed dismay, and he was instructed to be quiet. Martelino's testimony alluded to the fact that, even before Merdeka, some members of the Sulu royal family had planned to invade Sabah on their own initiative.

The real purpose of Jabidah was never made public, and even today speculation and controversy surround this secret plan. At that time there were various theories. Some political enemies of the president believed that the Muslims had indeed been trained to invade Sabah, as a special branch of the army. They even accused the president of having personal economic ambitions in Sabah. Others maintained that the special unit was to have fought Communists in the country, and so eventually the trainees would have forgotten the ostensible purpose for which they had been recruited. Another group believed that Jabidah had been part of a sinister plan by the president to create a praetorian guard for himself. Regardless of the real motives behind Merdeka and Jabidah, however, the massacre in Corregidor—the island that had come to hold a special significance for all Filipinos because of its role in the last war—created fear and outrage among Muslims throughout the country. In this they gained sympathy from other sectors of the population. One authority on the Muslim revolt in Mindanao has indicated the crucial impact of Jabidah and the Corregidor Incident: "As no other single incident had done since independence, Jabidah made all sections of the Muslims—secular and religious, modern and backward alike—concerned about their future."[5] Even beyond this, no single incident contributed more to subsequent events that led to rebellion than did Jabidah.

The Corregidor Incident was so heavily publicized by the media that it produced strong international reactions. Tunku Abdur Rahman and Tun Mustapha bin Harun of Malaysia voiced their opinions that the nature of the training program for the Muslim recruits signified Philippine ambitions in Sabah. Muslim associations and government officials abroad began to ask about motives for the massacre of Muslims by government armed forces without benefit of trial.

A number of blunders were made by government officials, and subsequent government action did not help matters. For example, platoons of young army recruits from Luzon were organized to march through the halls of Congress, avowing that they were the trainees who had been at Corregidor, and lo, here they were, very much alive. But when Muslim university students, who were present at the time to observe

[5]T. J. S. George, *Revolt in Mindanao: The Rise of Islam in Philippine Politics* (Kuala Lumpur: Oxford University Press, 1980), pp. 125–126.

what went on in Congress, asked the imposters in various Muslim dialects who they were and where they came from, the responses were only blank stares, for they knew only the dialects of Luzon or the Visayas. To offset this blunder, military authorities even pulled Muslims from the regular army troops and herded them in truckloads to a mosque in Manila to attend *jum'a* prayers. This, the army thought, would surely prove to the faithful that Muslims in the armed forces were not only alive but also encouraged to keep their faith strong and to attend congregational prayers. Instead of receiving sympathy, however, these Muslim soldiers were scolded afterwards by Nur Misuari, an instructor at the University of the Philippines, for serving as puppets of the army and thus hiding the truth about discrimination against fellow Muslims in the armed forces. The Muslim soldiers solemnly nodded their head in assent—and not without shame. Then they were cheered and embraced by the other Muslims in the mosque.

* * *

THE PRESIDENT AND the administration were embarrassed, for the army was obviously not managing its defense efficiently, and the scandal of the Corregidor Incident was reaching huge proportions. Thus, various segments of the government agreed to muffle the affair if not forget about it completely —for the cause of national unity. The congressional investigations and military trials ended with the acquittal of all the accused. A greater outcry was then raised by Muslims. Muslim youth and student groups organized demonstrations and rallies with visible support from opponents of the administration as well as from university intellectuals and student leftist radicals.

One such demonstration march originated at a local mosque situated less than a mile from Malacanang Palace, where the president and his family resided. A coffin bearing slogans on banners was carried by the marchers. Scores of demonstrators then squatted on the sidewalks bordering the palace and slept there for several nights, much to the consternation of the first family and government officials entering and leaving the palace on business. Perhaps more from concern about maintaining their popularity than from genuine sympathy with the students, Muslim politicians were compelled to loosen their purse strings to help finance the demonstration.

During this commotion, a certain university professor requested to see the president. An appointment was immediately set for him by a sympathetic staff person in the Office of the President. But because the president was occupied with an important conference, the first lady, Mrs. Imelda Marcos, met with the professor instead. The professor suggested to her, as she watched the demonstrators from an open window, that this protest march was unique in that it represented a new aggressiveness among Muslims. He warned that if the government did nothing to assuage the anger in the hearts of the families of the slain Muslims, and if it did nothing to help bring the legitimate aspirations of Muslims to fruition, then the wounds of Jabidah would never heal but would continually drain the nation emotionally and financially. The first lady emphasized that the president felt nothing but admiration for Muslims because of their renowned valor throughout history and because his life had once been saved by a Muslim soldier at Bataan during the Japanese-American War, and that he would never have caused the death of a single Muslim trainee —not even indirectly. She implied that political enemies of the president, within the country and abroad, were trying to implicate him personally in the Corregidor Incident in order to destroy him politically. The professor readily agreed that there was no reason to doubt the president's special concern and even affection for Muslim Filipinos. Surely then, he continued, there were persons or agencies within the government that were involved in schemes either without the president's knowledge or without his authorization as commander-in-chief of the armed forces. The first lady narrowed her eyes at this suggestion and silently studied the professor's face. She then stood and nodded: the interview was over.

For weeks after the demonstrations in Manila, *khutbas* would harangue the faithful, saying that the Jabidah tragedy not only reflected government insensitivity to the plight of Muslims but had also given a foreboding preview of things to come. Some Muslim leaders predicted that the government

would react with indifference again, should Muslims in Sulu
and Sabah shed each other's blood. They added that Muslims
were mere pawns, whether in the administration's plans or
in the independent intrigues of some government officials
who were harboring their own grandiose ambitions. Ironically, there were no demonstrations in the islands of Simunul,
Sibutu, and the nearby islands of the Samals, where families
of the dead trainees sat and wept over something they could
not fully comprehend. The military supposedly allotted a few
thousand pesos as an indemnity for each of the victims' families. It was rumored, however, that only a portion of the sum
for each family was actually delivered: the rest was pocketed
by the disbursing officers.

In January 1975, the above-mentioned university professor
had the opportunity to meet Nur Misuari in Mecca. Misuari
told the professor that his own political career was born during those nights when, in front of Malacanang Palace, he and
some fellow demonstrators had kept vigil over an empty coffin
marked "Jabidah."

* * *

ON MAY 1, 1968, Datu Udtog Matalam announced the establishment of the Muslim Independence Movement (MIM),
which would work toward gaining independence for Mindanao and Sulu. The clan of this *datu* had ruled the upper valley
region of the Pulangi, the largest river in Cotabato. In his
younger days, Datu Matalam and his family had welcomed
the Christian settlers and had provided them with farming
equipment. During the Japanese-American War, he had been
a famous guerrilla leader; also, he had once served as governor
of Cotabato. Now in 1968, he was approaching his seventieth
year and could be seen peacefully planting fields on his big
farm. Government officials began to wonder about his motives
when he established the MIM. Probably he meant to capitalize
on the outrage over the Jabidah Massacre, and by perfectly
timing his announcement about the MIM, he would be able
to present the aspirations of Muslims nationwide.

No one wanted to aggravate or upset the old *datu*. It was

well known that he had experienced personal tragedy and was becoming more pious. The president himself tried to mollify the *datu:* in a private conference he took off his own gold watch and gave it to the old man as a gesture of personal affection. But other forces were at work. Muslim professionals and students, some with leftist tendencies, encouraged the "grand old man" to stay firm and assured him of their cooperation. He returned the gold watch with expressions of gratitude but explained to the president that his people might believe he had accepted a government bribe. He continued to issue manifestos and to propose laws, written in the style of legal briefs.

Regardless of the motives of Datu Matalam, his movement revived memories of Muslim freedom and independence in the past, and his admirers spread beyond his close circle of followers. His influence caused concern among the settlers and the Christian population in Cotabato, especially among those with political ambitions. To assure them that they could also be included in the envisioned independent state, the Muslim Independence Movement was now changed to the Mindanao Independence Movement (still MIM). Like most other *datus*—and certain powerful political leaders who were virtually *datus* in every way but in name—Datu Matalam had his circle of armed followers, for this was a customary practice at that time. And because of both the special reciprocal relationship between *datus* and followers that was unique among the Muslims, and the intricately tight interconnections among the prominent Maguindanao families, Datu Matalam could expect the support of certainly several thousand—a force that, if armed, could pose a serious challenge to the government.

But Christian politicians in Cotabato also had their armed followers; further, the settlers, anticipating trouble, had formed armed bands to protect themselves. Groups of Christian and Muslim families began to transfer to safer areas, abandoning their farms and selling their animals and equipment. Enterprising individuals were making money from this refugee situation. Still there was no war for independence—no army of *mujahidin* swept across the lush plains of Cotabato. And still, the old *datu* could be seen working on his farm after the early prayer every day.

Yet something was about to happen. Trained and armed groups of nonresident Christian Visayans were seen in increasing numbers in Christian settlements and towns and near the offices or homes of Christian politicians. Meanwhile, rumors that young Muslims were being trained in Malaysia were arousing apprehension among Philippine government and military officials. These rumors seemed well founded when it was noticed that training camps were forming whenever these men returned home after brief periods of unexplained absence. It was becoming more obvious that foreign influences were at work, either to protect the integrity of the Muslim community in the Philippines or to embarrass the government.[6] As usual, more armed forces were sent to Cotabato and Lanao: again, the government was overreacting to a simple problem of law and order.

In 1970 there was a proliferation of paramilitary units: some were attached to the Christian mayors and politicians, and some to the Muslim leaders. Bands of outlaws roved the countryside. Early in the year, there was a violent encounter between Christian loggers and Muslims, followed by reprisals and counterreprisals. The Muslims generally resented the logging companies, which were owned by capitalists in Manila who through their influence finagled concessions from the government. The Manila press showed no sympathy for these companies either: it called them "carpetbaggers."

Age-old tensions built and erupted into open conflict in many places. In March 1971, a Visayan settler, Feliciano Lucas —nicknamed "Toothpick"—led a band of Tiruray tribesmen

---

[6] It is believed that the Muslim youths were trained in Sabah and at a camp in West Malaysia. At this time, the chief minister of Sabah was Tun Mustapha bin Harun, a Tausug who had been a famous guerrilla leader in the Philippines. Muslim traditional leaders in Mindanao and Sulu were often in contact with him, and no one disputes now that he was instrumental in helping conduct the training program. It is alleged that Tun Mustapha once considered promoting the formation of Sulu and Sabah into a single independent state. For details see ibid., pp. 234–238, 264. A high-ranking Malaysian official once remarked that it was difficult to control the amount of Tun Mustapha's aid to the Tausugs in Sulu, since he had many relatives there.

to the town of Upi in North Cotabato, and they killed about
six Muslims and wounded others. The Tirurays are an ani-
mistic people who in the past paid tribute to Muslim *datus*.
Their attack on Upi was explained as revenge for such past
exploitation. The true significance of this incident, however,
appeared later when it was revealed that Manuel Tronco, a
former constabulary officer with aspirations of becoming mayor
of Upi, was a close friend of Lucas; possibly he had persuaded
Lucas to launch the attack that was meant to drive the Muslims
out of Upi.

The Upi incident set a pattern for further attacks throughout
Cotabato and Lanao, in which well-trained and uniformed
guerrilla bands using sophisticated weapons drove Muslims
from the towns with ease. In retrospect, it can be surmised
that these terrorist activities were meant to ensure victory for
Christian mayors in the upcoming November 1971 elections.
Because the original group of Tirurays who attacked Upi
were called "Ilagas," the name came to designate any well-
organized Christian terrorist band.[7] As a rule, however, these
were composed mostly of Visayans. There was a strong belief
that these Ilaga bands were initiated by seven Christian politicians—"the Magnificent Seven"—who were bent upon pre-
serving their power and extending it further by infiltrating
traditionally Muslim territories. Manuel Tronco of Upi was
a member of this political group. Not to be outdone, Muslims
counterbalanced this group with their "Blackshirts" and "Barracudas," who also wore uniforms. Since the Blackshirts were

[7]In June 1971, a Muslim association published the following about Ilagas:
"Reliable information reveals that ILAGA is derived from Ilongo Armed
Group Association, which is composed of 200 armed members, specially
trained for terrorism and slaughtering Muslims. It is supported by 'influential
Christian settlers and government officials,' including seven mayors, for
political, economic and religious reasons. Their mission is Operation ILAGA
or DAGA, so called to kill Muslims like rats. [*Ilaga* is Bisayan and *daga*,
Tagalog for 'rat'.] It alludes to the previous Rat Campaign, when the tails
of rats were bought by the government; therefore, every rat killed is deprived
of its tail. Similarly, every victim of the ILAGA Gang is maimed; his left
ear is chopped [off] if male and her nipples are slashed if female, as evidence
to receive compensation." The warnings of Muslim religious leaders to
Muslims that retaliation by mutilating their victims was against Islamic Law
was heeded only up to a certain point.

known to have operated in Cotabato, it was believed at that time that they were the military arm of the MIM; but old Datu Matalam insisted with apparent sincerity that he had nothing to do with them. The Barracudas, on the other hand, confined their activities to the Lanao area; it was believed that their leader was a Maranao Muslim politician. The formation of these various paramilitary groups solidly established conflict between Muslims and Christians in Mindanao. In addition, there were instances of skirmishes between Christian settlers and neighboring non-Muslim tribesmen. The constabulary always intervened on behalf of the Christian settlers. Often the president also had to intervene to spare the tribesmen from annihilation.

It must be emphasized that most so-called Ilaga bands had similar motives and modes of operation—which might imply that they were organized and directed by a central authority. But not all Christian armed bands were centrally organized and so, technically, should not be considered Ilagas. Some of these groups were isolated, independent, and hastily formed to protect the settlers. Likewise, there were many independent Muslim armed groups who were connected with neither Blackshirts nor Barracudas. The fact is that, while serving to protect Muslims, the Blackshirts and Barracudas also served as power bases for their respective leaders in their frequent competitive countering with each other. For despite their common religious bonds, these leaders were also sometimes rivals because of tradition or ancestry or newly acquired wealth. Most, if not all, Muslim groups were extremely personalized and cliquish, and only an external threat common to all would temporarily thrust aside any rivalry among them. Here is an example of Islamic consciousness playing its part in forcing Muslim leaders to disregard their differences, if only for short periods. The *'ulama*, in turn, played a part in increasing this consciousness.

Because of escalated fighting by the end of 1970—Ilagas and Christian armed groups against Blackshirts, Barracudas, and other minor Muslim armed groups—there were other signs of discord everywhere. Schools in many towns had closed; farms were left abandoned, commerce had stagnated; the number of refugees was increasing. One report has given a very conservative estimate that at least 30 thousand Muslims, Christians, and Tirurays had left their homes for safer areas. Many Maguindanao families were given shelter by Maranao families: this number was not included in the report's estimate.

* * *

AN INCREASING NUMBER of towns in Cotabato came under constabulary control in the early months of 1971. One congressional team that visited Mindanao reported appalling conditions among the refugees and wounds in the community that would be many years in healing. Fighting did not end: on June 19, 1971, there was a massacre at Manili, a small *barrio*[8] in Carmen, North Cotabato. While most of the able-bodied males were out working in the farms, a group of about twenty armed Ilagas entered the barrio and asked the residents to gather in the small *nipa*-thatched mosque for a peace conference. Once they were inside the mosque, a grenade was hurled at the squatting old men, women, and children. Then the armed men began firing and hacking at them. Meanwhile, another group of armed men began firing at the houses of the *barrio*. A few Muslims were brought to the schoolhouse and gunned down, but at least seventy were killed in the mosque. Hundreds fled Manili and the neighboring *barrios*. The dead were so hurriedly buried that when a government team finally came to investigate a few days later, they encountered the terrible stench of human flesh, for dogs had already unearthed the corpses. The massacre was fully reported by the press: Christian reporters called the killing of innocent Muslims senseless. The foreign press took up the cry. Muslims abroad could not understand why innocent Muslim women and children had been killed.

The Manili massacre followed a pattern, that would be repeated again and again. It aimed at terrorizing Muslims

---

[8] *Barrio:* a village or small town attached to a plot of land; a unit of government in the Philippines.

in certain towns and *barrios* and forcing them to flee, at creating an exodus of Muslims. The Ilagas sometimes mutilated Muslim children, cutting off their ears or testicles: nothing was too brutal for them. Everything indicated that ambitious Christian politicians, who were preparing for future expansion of their power, were the ultimate culprits responsible for the massacre. The November national and local elections were approaching.[9]

It was through a British broadcast that Colonel Mu'ammar Qadhafi, the Libyan head of state, heard of the Manili massacre, and for the first time he showed deep interest in the affairs of Muslim Filipinos. An international congress of university presidents was held in Manila from July 11 to 17 to discuss "World Peace Through Education." There were two Libyan delegates—Saleh Buwaysir, the minister of information, and Dr. Shibini, the president of a Libyan university. Buwaysir had also been appointed by Qadhafi to serve as his personal envoy to President Marcos. In his interview with the president, at which he was accompanied by other Arab educators, Buwaysir expressed the concern of his president and of all Arabs for the plight of Muslim Filipinos. Later he informed Muslim leaders in Manila that he had told President Marcos of Libya's willingness to grant aid to Muslim refugees and that Marcos had welcomed this gesture. Buwaysir also revealed the Libyan government might donate additional aid for religious activities.

Dismayed and shocked by the massacre at Manili, Muslims raised a logical question: When Ilagas or Christian armed bands attacked a Muslim *barrio*, why would the constabulary take so long to arrive and reestablish law and order? For Manili had been under constabulary control and therefore under its protection. So why would the constabulary wait until the Ilagas had withdrawn before coming to squelch the attack? Yet, strangely enough, when Muslim armed groups took the of-

[9]During 1972, the year after the elections, many individuals known to be Ilagas returned to their homes. In March a radio station even broadcast that the chief Ilaga in the Manili massacre was in Bukidnon Province. Because of government apathy and the general breakdown of law and order in the country, nothing was done to the known perpetrators of the crime.

fensive, they often found armed troops of the Republic facing them. It was further noted that when Ilagas and Muslims clashed on the battlefield, the constabulary would suddenly appear and attack only the Muslims. Muslim leaders concluded that all this was not just a matter of Christian soldiers sympathizing with Christian settlers or the Ilagas; rather, there was collusion among Christian politicians, settlers, and some commanding officers of the Philippine constabulary in Cotabato and Lanao.

How were Muslim leaders to persuade the central government to stop this suspected collusion? One problem was that many of these ambitious Christian politicians were members of the Nationalista, the political party in power, and so were influential in the administration. Moreover, some of them— like Lieutenant Colonel Carlos Cajelo, a handpicked Nationalista candidate for governor of Cotabato—were former constabulary or army officers who had maintained influence in the military. The quandary of Muslims was indeed becoming more and more desperate.

*   *   *

EARLY IN THE evening of July 15, Muslim leaders—a senator, a former senator, congressmen, high government officials, heads of Muslim associations, religious and academic scholars and intellectuals, professionals and businessmen, and student leaders—met in a private house. After much discussion they concluded that if the situation remained as it was in the South, the very existence of the Muslim community was in extreme danger. Placing their hands on a huge copy of the Qur'an, they vowed to set aside whatever political conflicts and disagreements they might have had in the past and to commit themselves to protect all Muslims, regardless of ethnic and regional differences. They drew up a manifesto that included a list of complaints; they pledged before God that if justice could not be brought by legal or peaceful means, they would do their best to preserve their community and lands, regardless of their personal ambitions or political differences. The manifesto was published on July 21, 1971, in the *Manila Times*.

This meeting was important because, for once, scions of rivaling powerful Muslim families were willing to make their differences secondary to the Islamic principle of the preservation of the *umma*. For once, too, aristocratic families were willing to sit as equals among professionals and students of humble backgrounds.

Further, the meeting was important because among the signatories was a university instructor who would play an important role in the Muslim challenge to the government less than two years later. He was Nur Misuari, who had helped carry the symbolic coffin in front of Malacanang Palace soon after the Jabidah Massacre. He and others who signed the manifesto would become leaders in the Moro National Liberation Front (MNLF); others would become leaders in the Bangsa Moro Liberation Organization (BMLO). Some would eventually cooperate with the government in seeking a peaceful solution to the conflict in the South. Time, then, would reveal differences and conflicts among the signatories regarding techniques to attain what they believed constituted the good of the Muslim community in the country.

The July 15 meeting was important in yet another way: there was no talk of secession or even of autonomy. After all, some of the signatories were members of the political party then in power; a few were personal friends of the president; others were high officials in the administration or government agencies. Their manifesto demanded only that the government take action to stop the killing of Muslims and the loss of their lands. Unfortunately, the government misinterpreted their action as a threat to its authority; Malacanang was not at all pleased about the manifesto and rebuked some Muslim government officials for it. But the manifesto served an important symbolic function: it reassured Muslims that, first, their leaders could cooperate and act in unison as comrades and, second, they as a people were to be intimidated no longer.

* * *

NONETHELESS, SKIRMISHES BETWEEN the warring bands in the South continued unabated. In August, headlines blazoned news of the Buldon "battles." The town of Buldon in

North Cotabato was inhabited almost entirely by Iranuns. A proud and courteous people who loved their traditions, history, and mythologies, they generally kept to themselves. They conscientiously maintained a peaceful relationship with a Christian settlement that the government had implanted in their traditional lands. But they were not to be left alone as they wished. Iranun farmers were often shot at on their way to and from their fields. When one of Buldon's local officials was killed and his wife severely wounded, the citizens immediately rose to retaliate, for everyone in Buldon is related to each other by blood. Christian loggers in the area were killed. Expecting a counterattack, Buldon became transformed into an armed and fortified town. Interestingly, no Ilagas appeared to contest Buldon's countermeasure: perhaps Buldon had become too formidable a fortress, as it was situated on very high ground. Instead, the constabulary appeared in full force, but it immediately retreated when the commanding officer and two of his men were mortally wounded. Then the regular armed forces came, only to suffer casualties. Additional units were flown in from other islands. Meanwhile, some Maranao, close kin of the Iranuns, began to arrive with encouragement and supplies. Then the Blackshirts appeared to help defend the town, which now was well armed and protected.

Preparing for a carefully planned attack, the army bombarded Buldon with artillery for nearly a week. An ultimatum to surrender was then issued to the mayor. A general outcry of protest was raised throughout the country, since the conflict now appeared to be one between a large Christian army and a tiny picturesque Muslim town, and Muslims accused the army of attempting genocide. Christian and Muslim national leaders joined to persuade the president to intervene. So the mayor of Buldon was invited to Malacanang Palace, where he impressed everyone with his dignity and immunity to intimidation. With sincerity he told the president of his loyalty to the country and his pride in serving as a government official. He told others that there would be peace if the army and Ilagas were removed from Buldon. Eventually, after surrendering some of their homemade rifles, the mayor and his men were allowed to keep other arms provided they registered them with the government. The army withdrew and peace returned to Buldon. The colorful mayor continued to assert that he had never been a Blackshirt but was a loyal citizen of the Philippines, whose teeth were black from constantly chewing betel. (He spoke out against cigarette smoking, insisting that young people should follow his example and chew betel.)

In the following September, skirmishes between Christian Ilagas and Muslim armed bands were followed by the army's so-called search-and-destroy missions. Once again, Muslim leaders cried "genocide," charging that these missions were aimed only at Muslims, while the Ilagas operated unchecked in constabulary-controlled areas. Officials in Malaysia and Kuwait denounced the Philippine government not only for its bias against Muslims but also for its efforts to annihilate them. Qadhafi made the same charge and declared that he was sending aid to Muslim refugees. On October 8, *Agence France* quoted the Libyan leader as having said on October 7 that if "the genocide still went on," he would assume some responsibility for protecting Muslim Filipinos. He also said that he had sent an envoy (Saleh Buwaysir) to the Philippines to study the situation there, and that his envoy had confirmed the killing of Muslim Filipinos. The Philippine government protested Qadhafi's October 7 speech; then, on October 16, Buwaysir retorted with a public denunciation of the government, charging it with genocide, and called for the United Nations to intervene.

Meanwhile, two Libyan representatives had arrived in Manila with 250 thousand Libyan pounds (or 4.4 million pesos) in aid. A local Muslim committee was formed to buy medicine, rice, and canned goods for the refugees. Part of the money was used to buy a large tract of land in Quezon City, near the University of the Philippines, for the construction of a mosque and an Islamic center. The two Libyans toured some areas in Lanao and Cotabato and were appalled by the miserable conditions of Muslim refugees as well as by the sight of mutilated children, some of whom were later sent to hospitals abroad at the Libyan government's expense. Conditions were

so poor at these places that one Libyan visitor contracted para-
typhoid fever and had to be hospitalized for a month in
Manila before returning home.

   On October 26, a Barracuda unit attacked a constabulary
outpost in the town of Magsaysay in Lanao. A patrol of about
twenty soldiers sent to lift the siege was eliminated even before reaching the town. Then a strong army batallion was
sent to lift the siege and succeeded after killing at least sixty-
six Muslim Barracudas. This incident increased tensions in
the area. And November 8—the day for elections of governors and mayors—was drawing nigh.

*   *   *

THE ELECTIONS OF November 8 were ill-fated for Muslims:
many Christians were elected as governors and mayors throughout Cotabato and Lanao, and so the political power in areas
that historically had been part of the sultanates shifted from
Muslims to Christians.

   Another special election was scheduled for November 22,
since the vote counts for two Christian senatorial candidates
had run close. In the Lanao area at least 22 thousand votes were
at stake. Muslim traditional leaders and politicians were split
over this race, and there was even concern that it might incite
Blackshirts and Barracudas to come to blows with each other.
Fortunately, harsh rebukes from religious leaders and intervention by individuals with cooler heads prevented an armed
confrontation between both sets of feuding Muslims. Because
of the chaotic conditions in parts of Lanao del Norte, registered Muslim voters had been forced to move away from their
precincts, and so now they had to be transported in groups
to designated voting locations. In one particular instance, five
truckloads of Maranao voters headed for the town of Magsaysay, where they were to vote in the senatorial runoff election. Upon hearing that the town was under Ilaga control,
the drivers and passengers immediately decided to turn back.
On their way home, they were stopped at a military check-
point in the small *barrio* of Tacub. There they were ordered
by soldiers to alight from the trucks and lie flat on the road

facing down, ostensibly to be searched for weapons. They obeyed and were all shot. In less than a minute about forty Maranao lay dead or dying on the road. Bystanders and news reporters then viewed an ugly scene: some civilians wearing white bands around their heads—possibly to distinguish themselves from the Muslims—swarmed around the dead and kicked the dying to finish them off.

This incident made headlines, and the president ordered an immediate investigation. The findings of the National Bureau of Investigation resulted in charges against three officers, eighteen soldiers, a Christian mayor, and two other civilians. In less than two months, the charges against some of them were formally dropped; the charges against the others were soon forgotten. Likewise, the local press soon forgot about the whole incident. But the press in Muslim lands abroad did not forget what happened at Tacub. Soon after, in mid-November, three religious leaders—one from Russia and two from a central Asian republic—came to Manila and Lanao to visit Muslim communities "on a purely religious mission." Presumably their trip was financed by the Soviet Union.

By the end of 1971, the number of refugees, both Christian and Muslim, was more than 100,000. In the second week of January 1972, eight Muslim ambassadors—from Egypt, Indonesia, Malaysia, Pakistan, Singapore, Iran, Iraq, and Saudi Arabia—toured the Muslim South. They had been invited by the Philippine government to visit and see for themselves that there was no government plan for genocide. To the dismay of Muslim leaders and youth organizations, the ambassadors issued a communique stating that there was no genocide in the South. In fact, some Muslim organizations held rallies protesting the ambassadors' mission.

On March 1, the Supreme Council of Al-Azhar in Cairo —the most prestigious Islamic educational institution in the world—held an emergency meeting and expressed grave concern over the plight of Muslim Filipinos. Dr. Muhammad al-Fahham, Shaikh al-Islam and Rector of Al-Azhar, sent a cable to President Marcos on behalf of the Muslim Filipinos. He then sent another cable, on behalf of the Supreme Council, to the chairman of the Third Islamic Conference of Foreign Ministers (the ICFM), expressing official concern. The Islamic Conference was meeting in Jeddah at the time (from February 29 to March 4). The council decided to discuss the problem at the Seventh Conference of the Research Academy of Al-Azhar, which was to be held on September 9, 1972, in Cairo.

Because of the actions of Al-Azhar and Libyan representations, among other factors, the ICFM reviewed the situation, considering all the information presented by its secretary-general, Tunku Abdur Rahman. The conference then expressed "serious concern for the plight of Muslims living in the Philippines" and, in its Resolution No. 12, requested the Philippine government to guarantee to protect the lives and property of Muslims. It instructed the secretary-general to report on the results of this request.

On July 1, as a response to the above as well as to pressure from other quarters, President Marcos invited both Egypt and Libya to send delegations to visit the Philippines. The invitation to Libya was significant because Libya had not been represented in the ambassadorial team that toured the South in January. This delegation included Mahmud Hassan al-Arousi, the Egyptian foreign undersecretary, and Ali Trekki, then chief of the political division of the Libyan foreign ministry. The delegates visited some of the troubled areas, and, on his way home, Ali Trekki reported to the foreign press that the Muslims there perceived the "war" in the South to be a religious one, although he believed it was not. Members of the delegation had reported earlier that there was no strong evidence of a state-supported genocide but commented that, in any case, there was clearly a war between Christians and Muslims.

＊   ＊   ＊

THERE WERE NO large-scale skirmishes or "massacres" during the first half of 1972. The Ilagas seemed to have suspended their efforts to expel the Muslim population from the southern border of Lanao del Sur. Reports spread that they were now transferring their activities to other provinces, such as Zamboanga del Sur, where there was a Tausug minority. The Tausugs of Sulu challenged the Ilagas to come fight them in Sulu, and some prepared to sail to Zamboanga and help their brothers there should they be needed. Ilagas in Cotabato denied that the Ilagas in Zamboanga were true Ilagas. Ilaga activities in Cotabato and Lanao were diminishing. Possibly they had already performed their function there, since almost all the Christian candidates had won in the November elections. Moreover, the Ilagas were beginning to embarrass Christian politicians. Many Ilagas apparently were now unemployed and were extorting cash and goods from Christian farmers and small businessmen. Some enraged settlers even murdered a few of them.

Nor did the Muslims wish to provoke the settlers or the army unnecessarily. Yet there were ominous reports of new Muslim training camps, of newly arrived sophisticated weapons, and of the Muslims' increasing skill in handling weaponry. It became evident to many that the Muslim trainees abroad had returned and were now training others. This may be another reason why the Ilagas' enthusiasm had waned: many of them would prefer now to be in safer provinces, narrating their past exploits.

At the Seventh Conference of the Research Academy of Al-Azhar held on September 9, Muhammad al-Fahham strongly condemned the "genocide in the Philippines." The conference passed a resolution expressing grave concern over the situation of Muslim Filipinos. A copy of the resolution was sent to King Faisal of Saudi Arabia.

On September 21, 1972, President Marcos declared martial law. The administration gave many reasons for this action: Communist subversion, a rightist conspiracy, the government's growing impotence in implementing reforms, widespread student unrest. Another reason given was the Muslim "secessionist movement" in the South. However, it was a belief in some quarters that the president had already been contemplating the imposition of martial law for quite some time. This is why he had done nothing in the past to see that justice was done in connection with the Tacub incident or with similar incidents in which armed forces had sided with Christians against Muslims: he simply had not wished to alienate the army, whose support he needed to enforce martial law.

One of the first things the government did after declaring martial law was to order all illegal or loose arms to be given over to the authorities. But most of the Muslim private armed groups refused to surrender their arms because of their history of continual wars, their fear of army retaliation, and their unarmed exposure to Christian terrorist attacks. Moreover, they had already invested in the purchase of the arms (some of which had been bought from army personnel). The army's move to confiscate arms and ammunition in the *barrios* and inland towns of Sulu caused resistance and sporadic fighting. The announcement of an October 25 deadline for the surrender of all arms contributed to the so-called Marawi Uprising.

On October 21, at least five hundred Maranaos attacked the constabulary headquarters and the Mindanao State University in Marawi. Calling themselves the Mindanao Revolutionary Council for Independence, they included members of various dissident groups of disgruntled former police officers, restless students, former outlaws, religious scholars, and many young Maranaos. The rebels took control of the radio station at the university and broadcast a request to the people to support them against a regime that was bent upon oppressing Muslims and eradicating Islam from the country. Within a few days, government forces gained control of the city, and the rebels fled to nearby hills and forests, leaving behind forty or fifty dead.

It is difficult to explain this odd combination of such diverse groups, except that it was fear that led them to join and do what they did. The bulk of the population of Marawi did not support the rebels; but then, they did not know what was happening during most of the uprising. Eventually, most if not all uprising ringleaders were pardoned by the government and ended up in government jobs. But a few prominent citizens had been killed in the incident, one of them a Christian physician who had lived in the area for many years. However, his death was due to personal revenge, and many of the rebels were shocked and saddened to learn of it. The ultimate result of the Marawi Uprising was that most Christian families who had lived there for many years left, not to return—in spite of pleas from their Muslim neighbors. Similarly, Muslim families in nearby Iligan left for fear of Christian reprisals. After the incident, many Christian government officials of nearby provinces, Christian faculty members of the university in Marawi, and high officials in the then Department of Education and Culture in Manila tried to persuade the president to transfer the university to another province. The president refused to do this, as properly advised.

CHAPTER FIVE

THE MORO NATIONAL
LIBERATION FRONT
* * *

IT WAS AFTER the declaration of martial law that the MNLF
came into prominence. After the Jabidah Massacre, a few
young intellectuals, including university students, agreed that
the Muslim community in the country would be best preserved if a strong armed force were ready to protect it and
if it were explicitly stated in the national laws that in certain
areas the Muslims were to predominate politically and economically. But it was obvious that the constabulary and other
segments of the Philippine armed forces continued to favor
the settlers and that the central government was not doing anything to rectify the situation. Some of these young Muslims,
therefore, began to believe that only through secession and

independence from the rest of the country would Muslims be able to preserve their identity, to realize their aspirations, and to develop the economic resources of their rich lands for the benefit of future generations. Some of the leaders of the MNLF had been among the trainees sent abroad; upon their return, they were already laying plans for the future. They had gone under the patronage of the old traditional leaders, who had contacts abroad. These traditional leaders had always claimed certain prerogatives in their relationship with the trainees; but now they found it especially difficult to appreciate or understand the independence of mind of the returned trainees. It was not just a matter of poor communication between generations: rather, some of the young men had adopted radical ideas in the halls of Manila universities, coming to believe that the old traditional structure—which they called "feudal"—was a hindrance to Muslims' progress.

Among the most prominent leaders of the MNLF was Nur Misuari, who had graduated from the University of the Philippines with a degree in political science and then had stayed on as an instructor. Later he became a faculty member of the university's Asian Center. He was from Sulu, of humble family origin. Another leader was Hashim Salamat from Cotabato, who had studied at Arabic and Islamic institutions in Cairo. Salamat was related to influential Maguindanao families. The most prominent Maranao among the leaders of the MNLF was Abul Khair Alonto, a university student, and a descendant of sultans in Lanao.

So leaders of the MNLF represented all ethnolinguistic and regional groups. When martial law was declared, some of them—including Misuari[10]—were stranded in Manila. But they managed to reach the South.

During attempts to confiscate arms in the interior of Sulu, army troops were often ambushed or forced to retreat. On one occasion, more than one thousand soldiers were attacked, resulting in a great loss of men and supplies. Reports of army

[10]After the declaration of martial law, the Philippine armed forces placed a reward of 50,000 pesos for Misuari's capture—dead or alive—as the chief rebel leader. At that time, this was considered among the highest rewards offered for capture of an "outlaw."

victories were notably absent from the newspapers, whereas reports of an increase of Muslim rebels with sophisticated weapons were spreading. Because of initial successes, the MNLF's influence among Muslim armed groups grew, and they acknowledged its nominal leadership at least. In early 1973, it was officially estimated that the military arm of the MNLF—the Bangsa Moro Army (BMA)—had about 15 thousand men and would count on more than twice that number if the traditional leaders were persuaded to support it. In Mindanao and Sulu, the army had at least 10 thousand troops, which were supported by an additional 30 thousand armed civilians, mostly settlers.

In mid-March, while the army was busy fighting various well-armed MNLF groups in Zamboanga, the MNLF struck about twelve municipalities in Cotabato and occupied them for some time. In places where the constabulary and police had been especially abusive in the past, the Muslims' counteroffensive now was so vehement that more than a few soldiers were beheaded. This large-scale attack, which revealed the MNLF's ability to coordinate with precision and expand its operations, caused deep concern in army quarters because it was not at all like the attacks by private armies of the traditional Muslim warlords, by bandits, or by isolated disgruntled groups—attacks that had been sporadic, localized, often disorganized. By this time, too, the MNLF had already established propaganda groups in Muslim countries abroad.

The Fourth Islamic Conference of Foreign Ministers (ICFM) was held in Benghazi, Libya, from March 24 to March 27, 1973. In its Resolution No. 4, the ICFM again expressed deep concern over the "reported repression and mass extermination of Muslims in the South Philippines" and asked the Philippine government to protect the Muslims and to help return the refugees to their homes. The resolution also suggested that a delegation of four foreign ministers—from Libya, Saudi Arabia, Senegal, and Somalia—be sent to the Philippines to discuss the Muslim situation there with the government. Further, it recommended the creation of a Fund to help the Muslims, which would be financed by Muslim countries. In addition, the resolution urged all peace-loving states to use their influence to persuade the Philippine government to halt its campaign of violence against the Muslims and to adhere to the Universal Declaration of Human Rights.

The Philippine government objected to this proposed visit by the so-called Committee of Four if the delegates intended to interfere with the internal affairs of the country. However, in a letter to the secretary-general of the ICFM dated May 31, 1973, President Marcos said he would not object to the delegates' visit if they intended to strengthen friendship and cooperation between his government and those of other Muslim countries. In response, the secretary-general wrote to the president assuring him that the aim of the proposed mission was not only to find a peaceful solution to the problems of Muslims, but also to cement better relations between Muslim countries and the Philippines.

On August 14, the four foreign ministers—Abdul Ati al-'Obeidi of Libya, Mustafa Sise of Senegal, Omar Saqqaf of Saudi Arabia, and Omar Arteh Ghalib of Somalia—arrived in Manila. They announced they had come to help the president find a solution to the Muslim problem and bring peace to the South. However, before his arrival in Manila, Omar Saqqaf said in a press interview at Kuala Lumpur that he planned to request that the Philippine government treat the Muslims as it treated other Philippine citizens. The ministers were allowed free access to troubled areas, and all were eventually decorated by President Marcos. Meanwhile, the first lady formed the Relief Committee for the South. A spirit of optimism pervaded everywhere, and hopes arose that peace would eventually return.

When Ghalib of Somalia was in Jeddah on his return home, he commented that the Muslim uprising in the Philippines was Islamic in nature and not at all infected by any foreign ideology (namely, communism). He also commented on the good will of President Marcos.

*   *   *

ON FEBRUARY 6, 1974, there was large-scale fighting between government troops and the MNLF in Jolo, the capital of Sulu Province. It resulted in the almost total destruction of the town. A few days earlier, army patrols had attempted a systematic search for arms in various Sulu *barrios* and settlements. Most of the soldiers had to withdraw because of ambuscades. MNLF forces were then able to occupy two major towns, one of which was Maimbung, once a capital of Sulu sultans. On the evening of February 6, nearly one thousand MNLF rebels attacked the Jolo airport as well as all army camps and outposts in the area. Not until the following afternoon were government troops able to mobilize fully to drive off the rebels and to nullify their initial victory. Tanks and planes were brought in to subdue the rebels. Meanwhile, three naval patrol boats continually bombarded the town, causing most of the destruction. The MNLF troops were forced to retreat to the island's interior.

All sides generally agreed that the MNLF attack on Jolo had been disciplined and well organized and that its subsequent retreat had been orderly. Witnesses testified that army soldiers, on the other hand, had looted many jewelry shops in the town. Losses on both sides were heavy. Hundreds of soldiers, MNLF rebels, and civilians were killed. The fighting made an impression on the delegates to the Conference of Muslim States, which met soon after in Lahore, Pakistan; and international Muslim religious associations denounced the Phillipine government, especially its army.

At the invitation of President Marcos, Omar Saqqaf, the Saudi Arabian foreign minister, visited the Philippines from March 8 to March 14. Saqqaf held various discussions with the president, as well as with Muslim leaders. He promised the president that his country would help the Philippines financially in rehabilitating the Muslim South. In a speech to Muslim leaders in Manila on March 9, he said that Saudi Arabia was prepared to help rebuild Jolo, and he implied that aid would be forthcoming to the country "once this problem is solved." Upon his return home, Saqqaf made a lengthy report to King Faisal: it is believed that he tended to blame the Philippine army for the continual troubles rather than the president. In any case, the Republic of the Philippines was taken off the Arabs' blacklist of countries targeted for the oil embargo.

*   *   *

THE FIFTH ISLAMIC Conference of Foreign Ministers was held in Kuala Lumpur, Malaysia, from June 21 to June 25, 1974. The conference, in the preamble to its Resolution No. 18, referred to Resolution No. 4 of the fourth conference and stated that, upon consideration of the report of the four foreign ministers, it was quite aware of the sovereign character of the Philippines but was "at the same time concerned with the tragic plight of the Muslims."

As in previous resolutions concerning the Philippines, the conference once again, in Resolution No. 18, expressed anxiety about the Muslim situation there and asked the Philippine government to desist from killing Muslims and destroying their mosques and properties. The resolution further stated that the socioeconomic remedial measures proposed by the government were not sufficient to solve the problem, and it urged the Philippine government to "find a political and peaceful solution through negotiation and particularly with the representatives of the Moro Liberation Front in order to arrive at a just solution to the plight of Filipino Muslims within the framework of the national sovereignty and territorial integrity of the Philippines." The conference then appealed once more to other heads of states and international religious authorities to influence the Philippine government to ensure the safety of Muslim Filipinos and the preservation of their liberties in accordance with the Universal Declaration of Human Rights. Further, the conference members decided to create the Filipino Welfare and Relief Agency to improve the social and economic conditions of Muslims.

When the Malaysian prime minister had opened the fifth conference on June 21, he had made no explicit reference to the Philippines. However, Abdul Ati al-'Obeidi, the Libyan foreign minister, took the opportunity to remark that the situation of Muslim Filipinos was no less horrifying "than that faced by the Arabs ... in Palestine." The problem, he said, required not so much a social as a "political solution." The attempt by the Libyan delegation to have an MNLF representative speak before one of the working sessions of the conference apparently had not succeeded.

In a press conference on June 25, al-'Obeidi asserted that Muslim Filipinos "had been and were still [being] mistreated in their own country." Relief for them, he said, might solve their refugee problems but would not solve the main problem. A political solution was needed. He then expressed hope that President Marcos would recognize the MNLF. He expressed the fear that if Muslim Filipinos were not helped, their problem might get out of hand, and the Communists might step in. He added that at present, however, theirs was an Islamic movement—not a Communist one, as some Philippine government officials asserted.

There were various reasons for an increasing sympathy for the MNLF among the conference members. Many foreign Muslim officials had been bitterly disappointed by the chronic rivalries and differences among leading traditional Muslim leaders in the Philippines, many of whom were more interested in personal or family matters than in the Muslim problem. The MNLF leaders, on the other hand, appeared dedicated and willing to forego their personal interests in order to protect and defend the Muslim community. Libyan leaders in particular were impressed by their idealism and reformist ideas, especially those of Nur Misuari. But most importantly, the MNLF had demonstrated itself to be the best organized and strongest militarily of the Muslim armed groups. Libyan support for the MNLF was stalwart and unfaltering; and all the ICFM members probably would have supported all the wishes of the MNLF at this time, had it not been essential to avoid possibly embarrassing or offending Malaysia, the host country, which was doing its best to smooth over past differences with the Philippines.

* * *

ON THE BASIS of Resolution No. 18, Muhammad Hassan at-Tuhami, the new secretary-general of the ICFM, came twice to Manila for consultations in September 1974. These visits and others he made to various Muslim countries eventually led to the January 1975 Jeddah talks between MNLF representatives, led by Nur Misuari, and a Philippine government panel, led by Executive Secretary Alejandro Melchor. Melchor was well known in government circles to be sympathetic toward Muslims: he had always believed that a massive socioeconomic reform program for them was the best means of achieving peace in their regions.

As a prior condition to negotiating at Jeddah, the MNLF made an initial demand that the Philippine government grant autonomy to the islands of Mindanao, Palawan, Sulu, and Basilan as a single political unit. This demand almost put an end to the talks. But they proceeded, and the MNLF demands became more explicit: the autonomous government of this new political unit was to be vested with control over the internal security of its islands. Also, the new government was to be vested with power to accept any aid from Muslim countries for its economic, social, and cultural progress. The MNLF further stated, however, that the political autonomy envisioned for these islands was to be "within the framework of Philippine sovereignty" and territorial integrity. So MNLF leaders were now willing to abandon their former demand for secession or independence and substitute a new demand for autonomy they considered "significant."

Executive Secretary Melchor did not give way to any of the above demands simply because he was not empowered to do so. When Misuari asked that the Philippine constitution be amended to include certain guarantees for Muslims, the Philippine panel responded that the power to amend was not vested in them or the government but in the Filipinos. Ultimately, the executive secretary wanted to convince the MNLF that for once there was a sincere government effort to help the Muslims and to rectify past injustices. He hoped to arrange a truce that would stop the fighting and would enable government reform projects to be implemented without hindrance from the MNLF. He invited Misuari to return to the Philippines to join in the consultations and help implement the reform projects. Melchor believed that the problems in the Muslim South could be solved by Filipinos themselves—Muslims and Christians together—without military action or foreign intervention. He believed that solutions could be found through good will on all sides, not through further bloodshed and suffering. This was why he had included at least three Muslims on the government panel. Re-

liable reports tell that Misuari and other members of the
MNLF panel were even invited to head all government projects in Muslim areas, but that they rejected this invitation.
The MNLF also rejected a truce. When the talks appeared
to be heading toward an impasse, Secretary General at-Tuhami of the ICFM suggested that they be resumed in about
three months. He was doing his best to salvage the project
that he had initiated.[11]

* * *

SHORTLY AFTER THE Jeddah talks, the secretary-general
made his report to the Committee of Four. The committee
met in Jeddah from June 1 to June 4 and agreed upon a working paper consisting of a nine-point agenda for the second
round of talks. The secretary-general then sent the pertinent
documents to the Philippine government.

The proposed agenda contained not only the major original
demands made by the MNLF at the Jeddah talks, but new
ones as well. Some of the original demands were now explained
in more detail; for example, the agenda referred to an Islamic
self-government, a Christian minority in an Islamic land,
and to "good Muslim leaders" and members of "the Liberation Front" who would participate in the Muslim self-government as well as in units of "local security, defense and militia."
It specified under the category of "Defense and Foreign Policy" that all units of the special force of the Philippine army
and their bases as well as armed units set up "on account of the
war in the South" be dissolved. The new demands included
that an Islamic judicial and educational system be established,
and that the regulation of Islamic life and its institutions fall
under the jurisdiction of the Muslim self-government.

[11]The first formal meeting of the two panels was held on January 18. On
January 20, Misuari presented his four proposals, which he believed were
"the barest minimum that we can make." On the twenty-fourth, he ampli-
fied his concept of the Bangsa Moro State to at-Tuhami. Finally, in a letter
on the twenty-ninth, he expanded his four proposals into seven and added
that "what we really need to do at this meeting is for both parties to agree
on the creation of an autonomous Bangsa Moro State within the Republic
of the Philippines." In this last meeting, he was represented by one of his
advisers, since he was in bed with a fever.

Whereas the MNLF accepted the committee's agenda as a guide for the next round of talks, the Philippine government rejected it. It can be surmised that the government could not accept an agenda that it had not contributed to and that appeared to be one-sided, for it appeared to the government that the Committee of Four was acting on behalf of the MNLF. Whatever might have been the original intentions, the nine points in the proposed agenda seemed to the government more like demands than bases for discussion.

A more general reason why the government rejected the committee's working paper and agenda was that it questioned the MNLF's right to represent—through the demands in these documents—all the armed groups fighting government troops in the South. To prove its point, the government had earlier called together a "peace talks" conference for July 1 in Zamboanga City, to which more than two hundred rebel commanders and returnees, as well as Muslim leaders and government officials, were invited. Government agencies assigned to rehabilitate and reconstruct devastated areas of Mindanao and Sulu were also represented. A government panel revealed to those assembled the demands the MNLF had made during the Jeddah talks. As the government had hoped, many Muslims present questioned the MNLF's qualifications to represent them. In fact, they rejected Misuari as their leader and pledged loyalty to the government. The peace talks included a ceremony appointing Muslims as mayors, local officials, and heads of government economic and welfare agencies. Scores of rebel returnees were also ceremoniously inducted into the regular army. After these talks, the government sent special emissaries to the capitals of various Muslim countries with expressions of good will and explanations of its development plans for the Muslim South.

When the Sixth Islamic Conference of Foreign Ministers met in Jeddah from July 12 to July 15, the government sent a delegation, composed mostly of Muslims, to prove the Muslims' support for the government and to explain the president's plan to have four "autonomous" regions in the South headed by four commissioners. In spite of all this, the conference accepted—as set forth in its Resolution No. 10—the working paper of the Committee of Four as the basis for negotiations between the Philippine government and the MNLF. It noted with approval, however, the progressive efforts of the Philippines to grant more autonomy to Muslims while improving their socioeconomic level. But the conference also asked the government to desist from military action against the MNLF. The government responded by inviting the Committee of Four to visit the Philippines and see for themselves the improved situation in the South.

The Seventh Islamic Conference of Foreign Ministers, which met in Istanbul, Turkey, from May 12 to May 15, 1976, took a stand similar to that of the sixth conference. As expected, representatives from both the MNLF and the Philippine government also appeared in Istanbul to present their respective positions to individual delegates and to the Turkish press. To their embarrassment, some representatives of both parties found themselves in the same hotel in crowded Istanbul. Nonetheless, the Muslims in both parties did cordially talk with each other.

Despite government attempts to negotiate with the MNLF and other rebel groups, and despite comprehensive government programs for social and economic development, sporadic fighting between government troops and rebels continued. Fighting ceased temporarily, however, when a terrible earthquake and tidal wave struck western Mindanao in August 1976. For once, Muslims, Christians, government troops, and welfare agencies cooperated in their acts of mercy. Soon after, Ahmadu Karim Gaye, the new secretary-general of the ICFM, accompanied by foreign officials representing Libya, Saudi Arabia, Somalia, and Senegal, visited Manila and the devastated provinces. Faced with the vast human misery and destruction of property, the secretary-general announced the forthcoming release of the long-promised relief aid the ICFM had authorized in June 1974.

* * *

THERE WERE SEVERAL reasons for more and more former rebels returning home and surrendering to the authority of the government: the increasing effectiveness of government development projects, the appointment of more Muslims to offices at local levels, the government's general policy of attraction, and its offers of various incentives to lure the returnees back. This of course resulted in a weakening of the BMA, the military arm of the MNLF.

Then the first lady was sent to Libya in November 1976 to initiate a strong diplomatic effort to end the Muslim Filipino problem once and for all. At this time it was general public knowledge that the MNLF leaders were based in Libya, which was the main source of foreign financial and moral support for their movement. She was able to establish diplomatic relations as well as technological, economic, and cultural agreements between Libya and the Philippines. Colonel Qadhafi personally offered to help solve the problem and suggested that his country host the resumed negotiations between the Philippine government and the MNLF. These had been discontinued in 1975.

Consequently, another Philippine government panel, led by Carmelo Barbero, the undersecretary of national defense, arrived in Libya in December to negotiate with the MNLF. On December 23, 1976, both parties signed the so-called Tripoli Agreement which provided the general principles for Muslim autonomy in the Philippine South.

On December 29, the two parties were finally able to agree on a cease-fire as well as on certain general principles. The cease-fire was arranged by January 20, 1977, and talks were resumed in February and March.

But a sudden recess was called when the MNLF demanded that President Marcos declare thirteen provinces—Lanao del Norte, Lanao del Sur, North Cotabato, South Cotabato, Maguindanao, Sultan Kudarat, Davao del Sur, Zamboanga del Norte, Zamboanga del Sur, Basilan, Sulu, Tawi-Tawi, and Palawan—to be declared as one single autonomous unit.[12] To avoid an impasse, the first lady made a second trip to Libya on March 12 to solicit Qadhafi's help. On Qadhafi's suggestion, President Marcos on March 25 issued a proclamation (No. 1628) declaring autonomy in the thirteen provinces.

[12]This time the MNLF did not demand the "political autonomy of Mindanao, Basilan, Sulu, and Palawan" (a total of twenty-three provinces); rather, it excluded a great part of Mindanao, and so this new demand included only thirteen provinces.

However, since President Marcos held that administrative details for the autonomous regions required certain constitutional procedures, both heads of state agreed on the formation of a provisional government to head the regions and which would hold a referendum on how the inhabitants would like to govern themselves along administrative lines. A government report has it that Nur Misuari was offered to head the proposed provisional government but that he had refused. Qadhafi's desire to have MNLF representatives in the provisional government never came to be.

The president insisted on holding a plebiscite on the issue raised by the MNLF on the priniciple that this could be decided only by following certain constitutional provisions and procedures. He also emphasized that the majority of the total population of the thirteen provinces was not Muslim. The MNLF, on the other hand, contended that the holding of a plebiscite had not been mentioned at all in the Tripoli Agreement of December 1976.

On April 17, a plebiscite-referendum on many issues, including MNLF demands, was held in the thirteen provinces. The population of only a few of these provinces—Lanao del Sur, Sulu, and Tawi-Tawi—was almost wholly Muslim, that is, over 90 percent. The population of Basilan and North Cotabato was about 70 percent Muslim. That of Lanao del Norte, Maguindanao, and Sultan Kudarat, however, was less than 50 percent Muslim, and that of Zamboanga del Norte, Zamboanga del Sur, South Cotabato, Davao del Sur, and Palawan less than 20 percent. Of the total population of the thirteen provinces—at least 6 million—an estimated 3 million were Muslims, or about 50 percent. Since the majority of all the actual voters in the plebiscite were Christians, therefore, it was expected that the MNLF demands would be totally rejected.

Even many Muslims voted against the demands, Muslims who cared more about their own personal ambitions than about an autonomous government by the MNLF. These self-seeking Muslims had sympathized with the MNLF as long as it was fighting for concessions for all Muslims; but once benefits from the government—a grant of autonomy and political appointments—appeared to be forthcoming, these Muslims, who wanted to reap the benefits only for themselves, forsook the MNLF and would deny it any power. The government was well aware of this situation and knew it would be a major factor in the outcome of the plebiscite-referendum.

Another issue over which the government panel and the MNLF came into conflict was the nature and the control of the armed forces and local militia to be stationed in the autonomous region. The MNLF understandably feared that if Muslims had no authority or control over these forces, there could be no guarantee that past injustices would not be repeated or that peace would come.

Incidentally, some MNLF demands that did not pertain to military control—for example, that Muslims be allowed to hold high positions in the government, that an educational system be established for Muslims that would fulfill their religious and cultural requirements, and that a court system be established that would enforce Muslim personal and family laws—did not present formidable difficulties for the government, since it was already taking steps to institute these reforms, although slowly.

The MNLF was annoyed by the plebiscite-referendum not only because it was staged by the government with the aid of some Muslims, but also because the government had presented some of the issues to be voted on as "demands" of the MNLF, whereas originally they could have been intended to serve as bases for discussions or negotiations. Ultimately, the MNLF rejected the results of the plebiscite-referendum. Negotiations with the government were discontinued. Again, the MNLF began to talk of secession and independence.

The Eighth Islamic Conference of Foreign Ministers, which was held in Tripoli, Libya, in May 1977, discussed again, as expected, the Muslim Filipino problem. This time, Nur Misuari, as chairman of the MNLF, was allowed to address the conference. Many foreign ministers expressed disappointment that the long-awaited peace had not materialized. Other ministers believed it was necessary to encourage further negotiations between the Philippine government and the MNLF with the ICFM continuing to serve as the channel for a peaceful solution. The Indonesian foreign minister, in particular, emphasized the importance of maintaining the cease-fire. The result of all this was that the ICFM simply recommended that the negotiations continue. This relatively moderate ICFM stand brought relief to Philippine government officials.

CHAPTER SIX

RECONSTRUCTION, REFORMS, AND REGIONAL AUTONOMY

* * *

AFTER PRESIDENT MARCOS declared martial law in September 1972, the rise and strength of and popular support for the MNLF among Muslims forced the president to reevaluate their problems. Reflecting on the historical roots of the problems, he candidly admitted the chronic mistakes of past administrations and asserted that the country had "never really bridged the cultural gap between the Filipinos and our Muslim brothers, and it is for us now really to bridge it." He was beginning to realize that in order to reconstruct Philippine society, Muslim aspirations and expectations must be accommodated to the extent that Muslims would begin to feel as if they were citizens of the country. He affirmed that force should not be used in solving their problems. In 1972, the government initiated the process for improving Muslims' economic conditions, although slowly. In the next year this process was accelerated.

One of the first agencies created to rebuild devastated areas was the Presidential Task Force for the Reconstruction and Development of Mindanao. Other interagency task forces were created to rebuild certain provinces where there were large Muslim communities. Young, educated Muslims were trained to participate in these task forces. Recognizing at last the strong emotional reverence Muslims felt for their ancestral lands—not only because the lands held historical and sentimental meaning but because they represented the last economic assets Muslims could hold onto for survival—the president issued Presidential Decree No. 410, dated March 11, 1974, which declared these lands to be inalienable and not disposable. Subsequent decrees provided for relief and welfare projects, as well as for resettlement of refugees. In Metro Manila, Maharlika Village was created on land that once belonged to the army. Now it includes a beautiful mosque, an Islamic Center, dormitories for Muslim male and female students, a residential area—which will provide at least one thousand homes for Muslims when completed—the largest swimming pool in the country, and other recreational and religious facilities.

In 1977 the first lady ordered the construction of a beautiful mosque in one of the most important commercial centers in Manila. Alongside it is a reception hall, which, according to rumor, was erected in anticipation of a visit from Qadhafi.

Earlier, in August 1973, the Philippine Amanah Bank had been created for several purposes: to develop a larger class of Muslim entrepreneurs, to train young Muslims to gain banking expertise and more sophisticated knowledge of economics, and to help fund the rehabilitation of depressed areas in the South. In 1974, the Southern Philippines Development Administration (SPDA) was established to increase economic interrelations between Muslims and non-Muslims at regional borders. It serves as a program to develop techniques in business management and administration rather than as an employment agency. The government also liberalized the time-honored barter trade system between Sulu and Sabah.

Although the Republic is a secular state, the government began to issue laws and decrees and to create institutions that might at least preserve, if not strengthen, Islam in the country. These actions were intended to offset criticism from Muslim countries, as well as to assure Muslims that their faith would not be taken away from them. In one of his official speeches, the president went so far as to declare that the Islamic heritage was part of the cultural heritage of the entire country. Sometimes in less formal speeches before various groups, he would repeat a story about how his life was saved by a Muslim soldier during the Japanese-American War. To the amazement of guests at Malacanang Palace, yet to the pleasure of his Muslim audiences, he would claim with enthusiasm that his ancestors were Muslims and would blame Spanish colonialism for their becoming Christians several generations ago. The president had begun to realize that Muslims were not just interested in economic gains but that they had educational and cultural aspirations.

Consequently, the government authorized the use of the Arabic language in schools that might need or desire it. The Institute of Islamic Studies was established at the University of the Philippines, offering scholarships to qualified Muslims of modest means. The Department—now Ministry—of Education and Culture also dramatically increased the number of college scholarships for Muslims. Unlike the Commonwealth government, this government made certain that textbooks and instructional materials in public schools did not contain anything derogatory about Muslim religious beliefs or cultural characteristics. In 1980, the Ministry of Education began to study ways to help Muslims improve their *madrasa* system. The government now recognizes all important Muslim holy days and allows Muslim officials and employees to attend their religious festivals.

The president's approval of the Code of Muslim Personal Laws on February 4, 1977, was of great importance. As early as August 1, 1973, he had authorized the formation of a research staff for the codification of Muslim personal laws. The staff presented its work on April 4, 1974. On December 23, a presidential commission, which included Muslim lawyers and *'ulama*, was created to review this work and submit a more definitive proposal. The commission's work was completed on August 29, 1975.

The approved code deals with the most important Islamic provisions for marriage, divorce, and inheritance. It provides for a system of *shari'a* courts that is harmoniously and structurally integrated into the national system of courts and for a Muslim jurisconsult (*mufti*) to be appointed by the president. The approval of the code represented the government's recognition of Muslim personal laws as part of the national laws, although they applied only to Muslims. The code, in effect, can serve to educate Muslims further in the legal aspects of their religion and may, in time, reduce the strong influence of the *adat* in their daily lives.

Before the president signed the code, there had been some opposition to it from non-Muslims. It was opposition based not so much on the religious as on the legal aspects: most Filipino lawyers have been trained according to fundamentals of Roman law and the Spanish civil code, which favor a set of laws applicable to all members of the society. So they felt uncomfortable with the idea that some of their national laws would be applicable only to a particular group.[13]

* * *

THE CREATION OF Region 9 (Sulu, Tawi-Tawi, Basilan, Zamboanga del Norte, and Zamboanga del Sur) and Region 12 (Lanao del Norte, Lanao del Sur, North Cotabato, Maguindanao, and Sultan Kudurat)—which comprise ten provinces and contain the vast majority of Muslims—now signifies the beginning of the formation of autonomous regions

---

[13] One of the conditions made by the rebels of a particular Muslim ethnic group, upon which they would yield to the government's authority and give up their arms, was that the government must honor their recommendations that only particular judges serve in the proposed *shari'a* court system. These rebels wanted their relatives to occupy all the judicial positions, regardless of their qualifications. It is this sort of thing that has complicated matters for the government.

within the national framework. As a result, many qualified Muslims have been able to hold high government positions or to become more deeply involved in the political process. The original demand of the MNLF for the creation of a single autonomous unit consisting of the ten provinces of these two regions, plus three provinces in other neighboring regions —Palawan, South Cotabato, and Davao del Sur—is now a dead issue. It is doubtful that all thirteen provinces would ever opt to form one single autonomous region, simply because those who now hold political power in the created regions might lose their power if the provinces were restructured again.

Regions 9 and 12 are now demanding a more "meaningful" form of autonomy, with an administrative and executive machinery not initially envisioned for them or for any other region. As long as an autonomous region will not in any way pose a threat to the national sovereignty or territorial integrity of the nation or take advantage of its autonomy to engender seeds of future secession, the government in principle will not object to innovative changes within the region. There are specific provisions in the new Philippine constitution that allow local governments to devise ways to increase the public welfare; at the same time, it is a state policy that the government always honor the beliefs, customs, and traditions of the minority groups. Now that martial law has been lifted, it might be interesting to see how well Muslims and Christians in Regions 9 and 12 interrelate with each other and whether they cooperate in devising and implementing ways to increase their common public welfare. Considering the Philippines' long tradition of a highly centralized national government, however, we might question whether the kind of regional autonomy now in effect will fully satisfy Muslim expectations.

* * *

THE IMPORTANT ROLE that foreign Muslim countries and third parties, like the ICFM, have played in the struggle between Muslim Filipinos and the Philippine government cannot be underestimated. It was undoubtedly Muslim, espe-

cially Arab, sympathy and aid that helped push the MNLF
to international prominence. It was also pressure from Arab
countries that forced Misuari to shift his demand for secession to that of autonomy. And on the other side, the Philippine government exerted strenuous efforts to make Muslim
nations understand its position. While continually denying
the charge of genocide, the government often asked for time
to prove its sincerity in trying to improve the socioeconomic
status of Muslims in the country and in welcoming offers of
aid from oil-rich Muslim countries. It invited various secre-
taries-general of the ICFM, foreign official delegations, and
members of Muslim international religious associations to
visit and observe Muslim conditions in the country. It succeeded in forging diplomatic relations with Arab countries,
notably Libya. To change Malaysia's negative sentiments
toward the Philippines, the president publicly declared that
his country had no territorial designs on Sabah. Philippine
participation in and contribution toward strengthening the
Association of Southeast Asian Nations (ASEAN) led Indonesia, another ASEAN member, always to put in a good word
for its neighbor at ICFM meetings.

The Republic also succeeded in projecting itself as a country whose minorities problem, like that of other Third World
countries, was not of its own making but was a result of past
imperialist government policies. There is enough evidence
to show that many Arab countries—Saudi Arabia and Egypt
among them—were always opposed to dismemberment of the
Philippines: they wanted a solid, united Philippines bound
with strong ties to the Arab countries. But they also wanted
assurance that the Muslim Filipino community would be
allowed to preserve its integrity and that its leaders would
have a voice in national affairs. No Arab country would compromise on the matter of preservation of Islam in the Philippines. The government knew this.

As early as June 1973, when a delegation of the Rabitat
al-Alam al-Islami (Muslim World League) came to the Philippines to observe the Muslim Filipino situation, Sayyid Ib-
rahim as-Sagaff, an Arab from Singapore who headed the
delegation, stated both in private and in public that Muslims

should stop threatening secession. He said it was better that they remain a strong religious community within the Philippine nation. The delegation also included an Indonesian, a Malaysian, a Moroccan, and a Pakistani. They all appeared to agree with him. One reliable source reported that one of the reasons for his stand was that the delegation was upset by the bickerings and contradictory statements of Muslim leaders they interviewed. Before leaving the country, as-Sagaff made a personal donation to complete payment for a large tract of land in the environs of Manila where a mosque and an Islamic Center were to be built.[14]

The secretary-general of the Mu'tamar al-Alam al-Islami (Muslim World Congress), Inamullah Khan, took a stand similar to that of as-Sagaff of the Rabitat. He visited the Philippines several times and held discussions with the president and first lady. During the Jeddah talks of January 1975, he told members of the MNLF delegation to do their best to attain peace since the common enemy of the Philippine government and the Muslims was communism. He was often perplexed by disagreements between some of the traditional leaders and members of the MNLF delegation: after all, they were all Muslims.

The government's insistence on implementing its own autonomy program understandably frustrated and embittered Misuari. Moreover, several field commanders of the BMA defected to the government to accept political positions. One of Misuari's trusted legal advisers, Abdul Hamid Luqman, former municipal judge in Maimbung, Sulu, defected to the government in the middle of 1975. During the Jeddah talks of 1975, Luqman had once stood in for him when Misuari was in bed with a fever. With discontinuance of the resumed negotiations in Tripoli in 1977, it was inevitable that the cease-fire would be broken in some areas. So far, the MNLF

[14]This was land bought by the Libyan government at the end of 1971 for Muslims to build a mosque and Islamic Center. Money intended for the balance payment on the land was collected by a member of a prominent Muslim family who, after spending it for personal purposes, explained that he could not return it since it was spent on the "cause."

has not been able to match its field performance of 1973 and 1974.

Because of an improved image of the Philippines in the Islamic world and the diminished power of the BMA, the government grew bold and began to label any armed MNLF activity the work of terrorists. The newspapers ran stories about "Muslim terrorists," "Communist terrorists," and other unnamed "terrorists." Any activity by Muslim outlaws was often attributed to the MNLF.

By 1978, the long-promised relief aid from the ICFM had arrived. Within the next two years about thirteen new mosques were constructed and many existing mosques and *madrasas* were repaired or their facilities expanded with the relief money. Financial aid was also extended to mosques in Manila and some places in Luzon. However, no money was extended to victims of the August 1976 earthquake and tidal wave, since government agencies and private institutions had already provided them with a significant sum. To their credit, the Philippine armed forces facilitated the construction of mosques and *madrasas* by providing free transportation and materials, even labor. And some Christians, beginning to grow tired of the refugee problem and the conflict that had brought much suffering to both communities, showed sympathy by helping in the rebuilding of mosques and *madrasas*. Christian-Muslim interrelations on both national and local levels have recently improved.

CHAPTER SEVEN

RIVALRY AMONG
LEADERS

* * *

THE YEARS 1977 and 1978 were difficult for the MNLF
leadership. Some Muslim traditional leaders and old-style
politicians who had served in the Philippine Congress now
wanted to be recognized as the leaders of the armed struggle
in the South. Based at Jeddah, they bitterly resented the fact
that the ICFM had for many years consistently dealt with
the MNLF as spokesmen for the armed struggle and with
Misuari as the head of the MNLF. Often they would insinu-
ate to Arab and other Muslim officials and religious authorities that Nur Misuari was fundamentally a Communist who
was using the banner of Islam to cover for his own purposes.
Their insinuations succeeded to the extent that Misuari was

even called to appear once before the Rabitat; however, he was able to convince its highest authorities that he was neither a Communist nor a Marxist but a believer in Islam. One of the Rabitat members later remarked that he was convinced Misuari was a true Muslim, but his language just seemed to be influenced by Marxism.[15]

The above-mentioned traditional leaders had their friends and sympathizers abroad, as did Misuari. The differences between Misuari and the traditional leaders were so acute that their common friends often tried to reconcile them so that they might present a united front for the cause of Islam, or at least appear to do so. In such instances, all parties would appear to forget their differences; but once back at their bases, they would resume the usual recriminations. After Misuari convinced the Rabitat authorities of his commitment to Islam, he lashed out at some traditional leaders as enemies of the Muslim people of the Philippines. To say the least, this was probably not wise, since some of his sympathizers at that time, including those in the Rabitat, were allied to the established orders of their respective countries.

There is evidence that in 1977 the traditional leaders based at Jeddah tried to take control of the MNLF, or at least wrest it from Misuari's leadership. What resulted from their intrigues was that in the last half of the year, Hashim Salamat, a member of the central committee of the MNLF, declared

[15]While a student at the University of the Philippines, Misuari was a member of a leftist organization called the Kabataang Makabayan (KM). As the KM became more Maoist-oriented, he either dropped out or was expelled because his beliefs were not leftist enough. After some "purging" in the KM, a Maoist clique under the leadership of Jose Maria Sison took over the organization entirely. Sison became the head of the Communist Party of the Philippines and was later captured by the government in November 1977. Misuari was no longer a member of the KM when it fell under the control of Sison. The Philippine government and army, however, had often tried to associate Misuari with Sison in order to convince people, including Muslims, that Misuari was a Communist. To convince the government of their loyalty, some Muslims, in turn, disclaimed any connection with Misuari on the basis that he was reportedly a Communist. By intimating that Misuari was a Communist the BMLO had, ironically, joined forces with the government on this issue. All this is not to deny the possibility that Communist groups may have tried to contact the MNLF. At any rate, Misuari has been able to convince Muslim sympathizers in the Philippines and abroad that he is not, and never was, a Communist.

Misuari expelled from the committee's chairmanship. Salamat asserted that Misuari was turning away from Islam by favoring Communist methods and that he was losing the confidence of many of the BMA field commanders. He further complained of Misuari's increasing arrogance and secretiveness. Salamat, a Maguindanao, also happened to be a close relative of Salipada Pendatum, who was one of the most influential traditional leaders of Cotabato and a brother-in-law of Datu Matalam of the MIM. At this time, Pendatum was based at Jeddah.

Misuari counterattacked by expelling Salamat from the central committee and by introducing more members from the Tausug ethnic group. The traditional leaders tried to persuade Salamat to use Jeddah as the base for his MNLF faction. Sensing, however, that they were bent upon controlling him, Salamat returned to Cairo instead, where he was popular with many Muslim Filipino scholars studying there. It can be surmised that Salamat had strong reservations about some traditional leaders' commitment to Islam: he knew their main purpose was to control the MNLF through him. Like the royal Bourbons of history, these leaders could not forget anything or learn anything new. Descendants of sultans and accustomed to traditional deference and obedience, they could not tolerate the fact that other leaders, especially much younger ones, could take their power from them, overshadow their prominence, or deny them resources sent by sympathizers to aid the Muslims—resources that these older leaders believed ought to be theirs by right. They failed to appreciate a rising group of Muslim professionals who had minds of their own. Moreover, they could not tolerate the fact that some of these younger men, while holding their own personal ambitions, also had their own ideas and plans for restructuring Muslim society in the Philippines.

These traditional leaders at Jeddah succeeded only in accomplishing a split of the MNLF into two factions and the creation of yet another organization of their own, the Bangsa Moro Liberation Organization (BMLO). The two leading figures of this new organization were Salipada Pendatum and Rashid Luqman of Lanao del Sur. Luqman had once been crowned sultan in Lanao, and the government had contributed to the expenses of his ceremony and the festivities. Both Pendatum and Luqman had been congressmen in the Philippine legislature before the declaration of martial law.

The BMLO began to claim precedence over the MNLF. Among the reasons for this was that one of its leaders had assisted Misuari in the past and so believed he had been instrumental in the formation of the MNLF. At any rate, the BMLO failed to gain much support in either Egypt, where Salamat was, or Libya, where Misuari was. It was either purposely ignored or barely tolerated in Saudi Arabia, depending on the mood of the Arabs.

* * *

IN APRIL 1978, the Ninth Islamic Conference of Foreign Ministers was held in Dakar, Senegal. As it often had in the past, the ICFM recognized Nur Misuari as chairman of and spokesman for the MNLF. Hashim Salamat was unable to go to Dakar to represent his MNLF faction: it is believed that Egyptian authorities, not wishing to intensify further their friction with Libya, made certain he did not leave Cairo for the duration of that conference. BMLO leaders, however, flew to Dakar to make their bid to be recognized as leaders of the Muslim struggle in the Philippines. They weɪe utterly ignored. The conferences have continued up to the present to recognize the MNLF as the representative of the Muslim struggle and its leader as Misuari.

In December 1977, Abul Khair Alonto, a member of the central committee and one of the early founders of the MNLF, along with Misuari, made peace with the Philippine government. It is believed that he was persuaded to do so by his relatives: his father was a former Lanao governor and an uncle was the founder of the Ansar ul Islam, one of the largest Muslim associations in the country. One of his aunts is married to Rashid Luqman. His paternal grandfather was a Maranao sultan. Unlike Misuari, Abul Khair had generally supported significant autonomy for Muslims and had never shown much enthusiasm for outright secession. He stated that his main differences with Misuari were precisely on this issue. Had the army not harassed him in the past, and had it not then reneged on its word not to harass him further, it is possible he would never have gone to the battlefield. At any rate, Misuari dismissed him from the central committee. He is now a government official and is trying to improve the lot of Muslim Filipinos through parliamentary and other peaceful means.

* * *

THE CEASE-FIRE AGREED upon on December 29, 1976, has often been broken, with both sides fervently blaming each other. Since April 1977, there have been no direct negotiations between the government and the MNLF. The government has insisted that it wanted to continue them but that it did not know which Muslim group to negotiate with—Salamat's or Misuari's MNLF faction, or the BMLO. This was all despite the fact that the ICFM still recognizes Misuari as chairman of the MNLF and that the BMLO has become almost a nonentity despised by both MNLF factions. At one time there were indications that the government wished to transfer the forum for discussions on the Muslim armed struggle from the ICFM to the ASEAN. In March 1980, two members of the ASEAN—Indonesia and Malaysia—offered themselves as Muslim countries who would serve as "honest brokers." They apparently suggested that the armed struggle, although to be resolved upon the principle of Philippine sovereignty and territorial integrity, had regional implications that could best be resolved by the ASEAN. The ICFM's reaction to this is not known.

Meanwhile, Nur Misuari kept on trying to put military and diplomatic pressure on the Philippine government to force it to negotiate with the MNLF on the latter's terms. On June 9, 1979, he led a small delegation to visit Imam Khomeini in Qum. There he heard the Imam pray for Muslims in the Philippines. In the following October, the MNLF was delighted to learn that the Iranian oil minister had announced that no more Iranian oil would be shipped to the

Philippines if oppression of Muslims continued there. Although the country imports no more than 5 percent of its oil from Iran, the MNLF believed this was a good example for other oil-rich Muslim countries to follow. Needless to say, the MNLF was greatly disappointed when the Tenth Islamic Conference of Foreign Ministers, which met in May 1979 in Fez, Morocco, did not declare an oil embargo on the Philippines, after deploring what it described as Manila's violations of the cease-fire.

The discontinuance of the Tripoli talks in 1977 as well as the restrained resolutions of the ICFM led Misuari to accuse the Philippine government of a continued genocide against Muslim Filipinos. By this time he had reverted to his former position in support of Muslim secession and independence. In January 1981, during a summit conference of heads of state that was held in Taif, Saudi Arabia, Misuari tried to induce some delegates to submit a resolution calling for secession, but to no avail. The summit conference simply reiterated the old resolution that called for a just and peaceful solution to the Muslim problem on the basis of the principle of Philippine sovereignty and territorial integrity. The following May, when Misuari was in Jeddah, he contacted the Committee of Four—which included delegates from Saudi Arabia, Senegal, Somalia, and Libya—to convince them to support the MNLF's new demand for secession. He received no support, apparently because the demand would counter not only the Tripoli Agreement of 1976 but also all previous ICFM resolutions. Misuari reportedly then announced to the *Arab News* in Jeddah that he was going to work toward gaining the ICFM's support of his bid for secession in its next meeting scheduled to be held in Baghdad in June 1981.

✱ ✱ ✱

WHILE MISUARI WAS renewing his campaign for secession, a few things were happening in the Philippines that added to his difficulties. In September 1980, an apparently chastened Salipada Pendatum—one of the two most prominent figures of the BMLO based at Jeddah—arrived in the country. Avowing that he had never been in favor of secession but rather had sought a peaceful solution to the problems of the Muslims, he then publicly offered his services to the President and the government. Neither the government nor the military even questioned his past activities in the BMLO, which by then was practically withering. Then he immediately began visiting Muslim areas and delivering lengthy speeches: politics had always been his first love. The lifting of martial law has thus cleared the way for him to pursue his ambitions.

One of the consequences of Pendatum's return was the reactivation of the Muslim Association of the Philippines (MUSAPHIL), which had been somewhat dormant during the days of martial law. In the past this association had often effectively voiced Muslim goals and aspirations, and its congresses had well represented the Muslim people. Pendatum reassumed its presidency, which he had given up when he went abroad, just before martial law.

Sponsored by the MUSAPHIL, the Third Philippine Muslim Congress was held in Manila from April 30 to May 4, 1981, to discuss "Islamic Awareness of National Solidarity and Conciliation." The government had not objected to the congress; on the contrary, it had even provided facilities for it. Nearly one thousand Muslim delegates representing different provinces and segments of the Muslim population attended. According to the guest speaker—Inamullah Khan, the secretary-general of the Mu'tamar al-Alam al-Islami—the Muslim world supported "the rightful demands of their Filipino brethren for a meaningful autonomy in their areas." Various resolutions were developed—six of them important—and copies were sent to President Marcos, to the ICFM, to international Muslim organizations, and to Nur Misuari as chairman of the MNLF.

The first resolution informed the Philippine government and the ICFM that Muslim Filipinos accepted the provisions of the Tripoli Agreement as guidelines for establishing regional autonomy in the Philippine South. The second resolution appealed to the ICFM to urge the government and the MNLF to resume their talks on the agreement. These two resolutions together indicated that the congress delegates were not satisfied either with the regional autonomy in effect or with the extent of implementation of the Tripoli Agreement.

The third resolution authorized and empowered the MUSA-PHIL to act, both at home and abroad, as spokesman for Muslim Filipinos in matters affecting their welfare. This would provide a channel, or national agency, for ventilating Muslim needs and grievances to the government as well as to international agencies. Here it was revealed that there were still Muslim refugees in the country as well as abroad (in Sabah): the MUSAPHIL could act as their representative. This problem was further addressed in the fifth resolution. But although the congress, in its third resolution, tried to satisfy the urgent need for such a national agency to deal with the many problems of the Muslim community, it had indirectly subscribed to Pendatum's bid to be recognized as spokesman for Muslim Filipinos by authorizing the MUSA-PHIL to serve as this agency. Through the MUSAPHIL, he was determined to do what he had failed to do as a leader of the BMLO.

The fourth resolution authorized the MUSAPHIL to send a delegation to the forthcoming ICFM June 1981 meeting in Baghdad, Iraq, to present the position of Muslim Filipinos regarding an early, just, and peaceful solution to their problem. This resolution also stated that from the time the ICFM officially acknowledged the problem, discussions had been confined to those between the Philippine government and the MNLF. Here was clearly another attempt, therefore, to overshadow the prominence of the MNLF and to influence the government to deal eventually with the MUSAPHIL leaders.

The fifth resolution, like the third, addressed the refugee problem and appealed to the ICFM to activate the relief agency that had been created for Muslim Filipinos in one of the resolutions of its meeting in Kuala Lumpur, Malaysia, in 1974.

Finally, the sixth resolution requested the ICFM to urge the Philippine government and the MNLF to revive the cease-fire included in the 1976 Tripoli Agreement. Other resolutions included further requests of the government: to restore the writ of habeas corpus to Regions 9 and 12, where the majority of Muslims live and where, unlike in other regions, it has remained suspended; to implement fully the new law concerning the *shari'a* court system; and to strengthen the autonomous governments of Region 9 and 12 by making them constitutional bodies.

Whatever might have been the original motives for convoking the MUSAPHIL congress, it served well as a forum for expressing real and imagined Muslim grievances. But it illuminated certain things again. First, it showed the dissatisfaction, even among Muslims sympathetic to the government, with the existing autonomy, and it showed that Muslims wanted a more significant autonomy. Second, it revealed that the problem of law and order, aggravated by the behavior of the army, and the problem of Muslim refugees were far from resolved. Finally, it recognized the MNLF as a force still to be respected and heeded, and that Misuari could not be ignored as long as he remained its chairman. With regard to this last point, Pendatum reportedly said that neither he nor the congress ever questioned the legitimacy of the MNLF, but that he himself questioned that of Misuari to be its leader and spokesman. Here he was maintaining a position he had held during his BMLO days at Jeddah.

There was much brave and honest talk during the congress. Perhaps this was because Muslims are a spirited people not easily daunted by fear of the future. Their democratic discussions, coupled with a sincere attempt to arrive at conclusions or decisions by consensus, have always been part of their nature and traditions. Pendatum, because of his familiarity with the traditional Muslim institutions, as well as his extensive parliamentary experience, had to admire and support these traditional attitudes and methods. But just how well he was able to appease the government, if this was part of his original intentions, is another matter. At any rate, whatever investment the government put in the congress did not produce the desired dividends.

* * *

IN LESS THAN three weeks after the congress, the Philippine government sent two teams of Muslims to various capitals of the Muslim world to present its position in defense against accusations by Misuari—his "black propaganda" against the government. This was probably in anticipation of the June meeting of the ICFM in Baghdad, which Misuari and his delegation were expected to attend. The Muslim representatives denied that the government had violated the Tripoli Agreement by failing to implement autonomy. They disagreed with the MUSAPHIL congress that the form of autonomy the government implemented was far from satisfactory.

In June 1981, during the twelfth meeting of the ICFM in Baghdad, Misuari asked the political committee to support secession. He failed. Instead, the conference reaffirmed its support of the autonomy provided by the Tripoli Agreement. The conference passed a resolution, however, instructing Habib Chatti, its secretary-general, to renew discussions with the Philippine government regarding the implementation of autonomy according to the agreement. The secretary-general was also to report within three months to the Committee of Four, which had been created to oversee implementation of the agreement. As this resolution implies, therefore, the ICFM does not believe, after all, that the Philippine government has fully implemented the kind of autonomy envisioned by the Tripoli Agreement.

CHAPTER EIGHT

PROSPECTS: A PLURALISTIC SOCIETY AND PEACE?

* * *

CONSIDERING THE EVENTS through June 1981 and all the
efforts to achieve compromise, we can see that the Philippine
government will never allow the Muslims to secede or form
an independent state. And, unless coerced to do so, it might
never grant an autonomy they would find fully meaningful
and acceptable. So far, the government has granted autonomy
defined in its own terms only, or based on its own interpretation
of the Tripoli Agreement. And so far the ICFM has refused
to support Misuari's demand that the Muslims be granted full
independence. Instead, the conference members still support
the vague version of autonomy prescribed by the Tripoli
Agreement. They are not likely to change their stand in the
immediate future.

Moderate progress has been made, however, and certain concessions have been won. The most significant government reform and development programs to improve conditions for the Muslims were all initiated in the first two years after proclamation of martial law in 1972. Results became evident some time after the mid-1970s. Other changes have come about, and I shall note them as well as the implications of these reform programs. Also to be noted are problems that remain—the continued refugee problem and sporadic fighting. A future for the Muslim Filipinos can be speculated upon, but with uncertainty. It is a shaky future, which rests on a fragile foundation laid by their slow, limited progress and by the precarious gains they have won so far. Finally, a future for the nation as a whole can be speculated upon, with hope for peace and unity.

Indeed, a better future for the Muslims depends in large part on whether they hold on to and use the gains they have won so far. It is also crucial that they preserve the integrity of Islam and strive to fulfill the moral, ethical, social, and cultural ideals it embodies by putting these ideals into daily practice. If Muslim Filipinos commit themselves to these efforts, they can set an example for living that non-Muslim Filipinos might respect and even learn from. Then the rest of the nation might begin to value the Muslims and embrace them as fellow citizens.

Other Filipinos are beginning to realize that the Muslims in their country are not an alien people trying to take control of a region not their own or just another militant group, like the Communists, trying to take control of Malacanang Palace or the government. Rather, the Muslims are gaining recognition as a people with cherished traditions and deep roots in a separate history, with a special religious faith and culture that they have a right to preserve. External events not of their making, or choosing, have woven these people inextricably into the larger political body, the Philippine nation. And although a component of the whole political body, they cannot fully share in a nationalistic spirit with the majority of Filipinos, who are non-Muslim, unless they are accepted as equal in spite of their cultural separateness. They must be accepted as a people with ideals, values, customs, and social institutions that are different from but nonetheless just as valid and worthy as those of other Filipino peoples.

If domestic peace and coexistence are to have high priority as national goals, then a strong sense of unity and harmony among the various cultural and ethnic groups should ultimately transcend the nation's cultural and ethnic diversity, or "plurality," and prevail. But this will be difficult and will require committed efforts from each group. Some moral, ethical, social, and cultural values and institutions intrinsic to Muslim and Christian communities are often not mutually compatible. And at present, both groups are more aware of their differences than of their potential for interaction as members of a cohesive and balanced society.

Understanding the problems inherent in a pluralistic society is crucial to understanding the Muslim Filipino problem, their current sociopolitical movement, and the motives behind shifting MNLF demands for self-government or threats of secession. The Muslim Filipino movement must be viewed against the background of historical imperialism and the modern-day version of pluralism that it reinforced: two concepts powerfully charged with emotional implications. Then this Muslim movement and the reasons why it has involved military, as well as social and political, conflict will be better understood.

* * *

THERE ARE CERTAIN changes or trends toward change that have developed and may lead to progress for the Muslims: There are the recent political changes, including expansion of the president's executive powers by constitutional amendments. The government has enacted reform programs to improve the living conditions of Filipinos in general and programs to accommodate the Muslims in particular to the nation's administrative and economic systems; it has made some effort to guarantee preservation of the Islamic faith. There has been an increasing commitment among the Muslims to educate themselves better, to develop business and technological skills, and to raise their economic status. This has been accompanied by an increasing consciousness of their own identity as Muslims in view of the ideals and values of Islam and a stronger commitment to preserve traditions of the faith. Muslim Filipino leaders—especially the politicians and "moderates"—have shown greater awareness of the suffering and needs of their people; Muslims throughout the world have learned of the oppression of their brother Muslims in the Philippines. A general change of heart may be seen spreading through the rest of the Filipino population, including Christians; there is a definite trend toward accepting, respecting, and sympathizing with the Muslims in their country. These changes for the better have come about because so many Muslims have fought for them, with great loss of life. And the major force behind the ongoing fight for freedom has been, and still is, the MNLF.

*   *   *

THE EMERGENCE AND rise of the MNLF can be considered the important factor that compelled the government to face up to the Muslim problem at last and to work toward remedies. It did not take the government long to realize that the MNLF was not just a band of upstart guerrillas, but a vigorous ideological movement with Islam as its banner. The loyalty it has attracted knows no regional and linguistic boundaries. The MNLF continues to draw widespread support or at least sympathy. More than any other organization in the country, it has aroused international concern for the plight of Muslim Filipinos. The MNLF was able to gain—and so far has maintained—recognition by the ICFM as the legitimate exponent for the Muslim armed struggle in the Philippines, in spite of fervent bids for such status by other Muslim leaders and organizations. This is not to deny the significance of the others, including "moderates" like MUSAPHIL and the traditional leaders, and of the parts they have played in strengthening the Muslim community. Many of them have been consulted by or have cooperated with the government on programs they sincerely believed would benefit their people;

but their voices might never have been heard were it not for the MNLF's worldwide influence and vigorous guerrilla struggle.

At one time there was an amicable relationship between the MNLF and traditional Muslim leaders. Many staunch members and supporters of the MNLF are former supporters of the traditional faction; in fact, some of the most important MNLF leaders have been kinsmen of traditional Muslim leaders or old-style politicians. And until the two factions clashed over the issue of which was to head their people's cause, they needed and aided each other: the traditional leaders, for example, were instrumental in arranging, through their resources and contacts outside the country, for the first Muslim armed trainees to be sent abroad, and so indirectly aided the MNLF's birth.

So far, thousands of Muslim Filipinos have been displaced from their homes and farms—their ancestral lands—by Christian settlers sponsored by the government as well as by the recent fighting. Some of them have resettled elsewhere, but many consider themselves refugees. They will probably be unable to fully recover their farms. Anyway, it is possible that for the growing number of Muslims who are becoming professionals, entrepreneurs, and industrial workers, the close tie to the land might be weakened in the future. But so far the land still represents for most Muslims the last tangible evidence of their past possessions and heritage, and they cling passionately to the hope of regaining it. As long as Muslims who yearn to return to their lands are repeatedly provoked by the army or neighboring groups, strife and discord will continue. After all, for many of the refugees who were wandering and restless, joining the MNLF has signified their only remaining hope: a desperate last effort to retain a scrap of honor or dignity.

*   *   *

IT IS TOO soon to predict all the consequences of, first, the lifting of martial law in January 1981 and, second, the approval of recent constitutional amendments that have expanded the president's powers. These two changes may bring a mixture of blessings and problems to the Muslim Filipinos.

The lifting of martial law resulted in the return of some power to provincial and local governments but may also signify the return of the traditional Muslim leaders to their old powers and prerogatives. The return of Pendatum is an example of this change and perhaps signals a more substantial shift in power in the Muslim South, should other traditional leaders and politicians like Pendatum return. And should they be so busy politicking and protecting their own personal and family interests that they neglect the urgent social and economic problems of the constituencies they represent, the progress the Muslims have made will suffer a setback. Also, the past has often revelaed that some members of the *'ulama* —again, because of family and financial interests or personal ambitions—tend to attach themselves to the entourage of popular politicians. This is unfortunate, as a dedicated, united, and uncorrupted *'ulama* is needed especially at this time: they can serve to admonish those political leaders who have neglected their Islamic social responsibilities to the community. Then there are the younger Muslim professionals and business leaders who, if they do not allow themselves to be swayed by the political leaders to join their cliques as colleagues or aides, might serve to challenge the old politicians, keep them in check, as well as to influence and revitalize the *'ulama.*

During this period of change, therefore—characterized by the struggle and chaos that accompanies any shifting of power —it is crucial to the Muslims' cause that they be led by honorable and conscientious political leaders, a strong and dedicated *'ulama*, and young, energetic, and influential leaders in business and the professions. It can be argued, however, that only a strong, clear-sighted president, who uses his executive powers with the most benevolent of motives, who sponsors sound, progressive policies to benefit all Filipinos, and who is supported by wholesome institutions in the country, can ultimately restore peace to the South. But he must listen to the dedicated or unselfish Muslims and seek to meet their legitimate needs and desires.

Perhaps the president will use the additional constitutional powers recently granted him to curb the replenished power of self-serving Muslim politicians or to undermine their traditional "feudalistic" system of economics and local government. Traces of this kind of social, economic, and political structure remain throughout non-Muslim Philippine society as well, whereas it is still dominant in the Muslim society. Based on an agrarian economy with tenant farm labor, and landownership and power concentrated in the hands of a few—usually the traditional leaders and old-style politicians—the "feudalistic" system may impede the Muslims' economic and political progress if it is not held in check.

During the early days of martial law, there was speculation that an active rapport between President Marcos and the MNLF leaders, if reinforced by mutual respect, might paradoxically lead to elimination of this traditional "feudalism" in Muslim society. Such weakening of internal power bases would be to the president's advantage; after all, he had often announced his intention to eliminate the "oligarchs," as well as the traces throughout the country of the feudalistic "old society" that had established these "oligarchs," both Muslim and non-Muslim. But this theory is too simplistic and optimistic. First of all, the president has often relied on Muslim "oligarchs" to strengthen himself politically, although their power has been merely nominal for quite some time. Second, his cooperation with the MNLF might well have pushed strong MNLF leaders into a position of real power and national influence, and the president would probably not have tolerated real power in the hands of any single group. Nor would the army have tolerated an MNLF stronghold in the South, as long as the Muslims maintained an active military arm there. And as long as martial law was in effect, the MNLF, likewise, would not have cooperated with the army, which had abused and terrorized so many Muslims.

Were the Muslim areas granted significant or substantial autonomy under MNLF control, however, Nur Misuari had planned to achieve reforms that would eliminate the "oligarchs" and abolish their socioeconomic order that is debilitating to the Muslim community. Nonetheless, the discontent and instability—social, economic, political—caused by the "feudalistic" system of Muslim landownership cannot be dealt with as an isolated problem. It must be dealt with as part of a bigger national problem: that of discontent and instability caused by concentrated economic power in the hands of a few throughout the Philippines. Again, it is a problem that must be confronted by a progressive, benevolent, clear-sighted president who is concerned with restoring internal peace to his country.

*   *   *

NUR MISUARI WARNED the Muslim Filipinos never to take for granted any of their recent gains or any government benefits they had won. In a discussion in Saudi Arabia in March 1979, he expressed to me his fears: if pressure on the present government were eased or if a new administration more hostile to the Muslims were to come to power, many of the concessions the Muslims have gained might be withdrawn or nullified. This is one reason he has always insisted on explicit constitutional guarantees for the Muslims instead of mere presidential decrees or executive orders. He meant to wish the president not the slightest ill will, but nonetheless expressed deep concern for his people's future should a totally military regime take control of the country. His fears are shared by most Muslims. He was viewing the future as an extension of their past: theirs has been a history of continual warring against foreign armies trying to colonize them or against neighboring indigenous groups trying to displace them from their lands. The Muslims have long distrusted whatever regime sat in rule in Manila at the time, always perceiving it as a foreign imperialist government and its military force as a hated army of occupation.

Indeed, the omnipresence of the army in Muslim areas is not a good sign that peace is at hand. The Muslims continue to perceive it as an army of occupation in their territory, relentlessly baiting them, provoking unnecessary friction and turmoil. There have also been many instances of extortion from and brutality against civilian Muslims by the regular army or by "lost commands." Moreover, troops cannot always distinguish innocent civilians from members of the BMA. Usually poorly disciplined and unaccustomed to their surroundings, the soldiers tend to overreact, firing impetuously and sometimes without official command, only to discover their mistakes too late. This often brings retaliation from victims' families: individual soldiers then become victims of the revenge sought by Muslims for unjustified killing of their relatives. This, in turn, brings massive retaliation from the army; consequently, more innocent Muslims are killed, and so the vicious cycle continues.

Although there are now many intelligent young army officers with university educations who may be broad-minded enough to view Muslims sympathetically, their military training has dictated their loyalty to the army and has inspired them with a belief in a logic of force and bloodshed. So they often treat the Muslims as ruthlessly as the older officers do. Philippine army personnel, as well as government officials, often have difficulty empathizing or communicating with Muslim civilians.

On February 12, 1981, presumably MNLF forces killed about 120 army soldiers on Pata Island, which is a few miles south of Jolo Island. Policed by just a small constabulary force, Pata Island has always been relatively peaceable. A week or so before the massacre, however, about two hundred army soldiers had arrived, either to register the arms of surrendered MNLF troops or to disarm surrendering former rebels who had been formed into civilian defense units. Government reports assert that the soldiers had arrived to accept a formal surrender of rebels and were maliciously gunned down. Rebel sources insist that the soldiers were attacked because they had abused Muslim women, strafed homes of peaceable families, and desecrated mosques. Whichever report is the truth, military retaliation was severe. Massive land, sea, and air operations involving at least 15 thousand troops were launched. The civilian islanders suffered terribly, and of the estimated 15 thousand of them, hundreds of women and children were killed. Reports of the death toll—not yet complete—range from five hundred to over a thousand. The military asserted that some civilians joined the three or four hundred rebels and that others refused to be evacuated to the areas specified by the government. Survivors were not

104 The Contemporary Muslim Movement in the Philippines

allowed to return to their farms or to gather food and supplies and were suffering from starvation. Several thousand were eventually transported to Jolo. This incident demonstrates the severity of government retaliation following most clashes between the army and the MNLF: innocent civilians inevitably suffer. Yet administration officials always allege that victims, if not in collusion with the MNLF, are unfortunately in the wrong place at the wrong time, and that such incidents are beyond anyone's control or blame.

The Pata Island incident infuriated Muslim government officials. Some of them tried to persuade the president to withdraw all Philippine army units from Muslim areas or, at least, to replace them with Muslim soldiers, who would have better rapport with their own people and could perhaps be more successful in controlling them. But as long as Muslim soldiers are not trusted by high-ranking army officers, and since very few high-ranking officers are Muslims, such a suggestion will remain unheeded. Underlying all this, of course, is the unspoken assumption in all quarters that army withdrawal from any Muslim area would leave it open to immediate MNLF control.

* * *

REGARDLESS OF PHILIPPINE army attempts to suppress and intimidate them, the Muslim Filipinos are now more than ever in a position to defend themselves and to carry on their social reform movement. And, regardless of the Philippine government's ambivalent intentions and dilatory tactics, the MNLF, especially the Misuari faction, cannot be ignored.

It has been suggested that perhaps the peak of Nur Misuari's power and influence was at the Jeddah talks of January 1975, when he and his MNLF delegation confronted the government's panel sent to convince him to return and aid in the government's projects to help the Muslims. Those who have suggested this believe his power began to diminish soon afterward. But his faction includes the strongest and best-disciplined Muslim combat force in the South. And even if it

forms a coalition with the Salamat faction (which also main-
tains a combat force in Cotabato and Lanao in spite of recent
defections by its commanders), the MNLF of Misuari will
still be capable of launching and sustaining combat with the
Philippine army, and so will continue to cause considerable
strain on the national budget.

Some former members who defected to the army and suffered abuses there have returned to the MNLF.[16] And the
MNLF continues to recover some of its former members
who left for positions offered them in the government, and
then became dissatisfied. So there are signs the MNLF is very
much alive. Nur Misuari has prepared for a long struggle
and has reportedly already chosen a group of younger men
as his successors, to carry on the MNLF leadership after him.
These designated leaders have backgrounds different from
that of Misuari: they have been educated in Arab countries
and have been exposed to radical Arab organizations and
movements. They might therefore make even greater demands than Misuari has made; they might build the MNLF
into an even greater threat to the government than it has
been under his name.

Nonetheless, the MNLF has so far proved effective in pres-
suring the government to yield to demands from at least the
Muslim "moderates," if not to some of Misuari's demands.
Should new political developments bring serious unrest or
upheaval to the country, or should substantial financial aid
and other forms of support arrive from sympathizers abroad,
the MNLF would no doubt become a more formidable force
to reckon with, regardless of its leadership.

* * *

BUT BLOODSHED WOULD not be necessary if the non-Muslim
majority would accept the diversity inherent in their country's
cultural makeup; bloodshed would not be necessary if the

---

[16] According to the latest (1981) army reports, about 30,000 armed members
of the MNLF and other Muslim armed groups have yielded to the government. However, at least 10,000 MNLF "are continuing the fight in the
South for greater autonomy."

government would encourage this pluralism in the country and channel it in a progressive direction. In a truly pluralistic society, different cultural groups, while maintaining their cultural identities, all share in the national power and, in spite of criss-crossing loyalties, all are held together by a common loyalty to a wider community—that of the nation. Here a question may arise whether, in spite of different cultures, a national culture can exist that will represent cultural goals of another type and a higher level. Also, how can this national culture, while transcending diverse local cultures, be enriched by these cultures?

Actually, when the Spaniards came to the Philippines in the sixteenth century, they met many different and widely scattered ethnic and cultural groups. They tried to impose their social values, cultural and religious institutions, and economic system on the indigenous peoples they subjected. The twofold aim of the Spanish conquest was the Christianization of the natives and the extension of the economic interests of the Spanish king. The Spaniards succeeded in integrating most of the natives into a community that was both political and ecclesiastical. The vast majority of the natives became Christians as well as subjects of the Spanish monarch. But the Spaniards never really succeeded in assimilating the Muslims and their sultanates into the above community. They failed to transform the *moros* into Christian *indios*.

The Filipino nationalist movement represented the attempt of the Christianized or Westernized *indios* to wrest political power from Spanish colonial authorities. The *indios* wanted to be called "Filipinos" and contested the application of this term to refer exclusively to Spaniards born in the Philippines. They had no intention of returning to a former nativistic culture or giving up Christian values that they and their ancestors had adopted and learned to cherish. Once Christian Filipinos inherited the imperial mantle, they treated the Muslims in the Philippines in almost the same manner that the Spaniards and Americans had. Filipino nationalist leaders adopted a colonial stance toward the Muslims. This explains why for the last so many decades the Muslims have regarded the Manila government as no different from that of the Spanish or American colonial governments. The Muslims did not participate in the so-called nationalist movement against Spain. For various historical reasons, however, they with other cultural minorities found themselves in a body politic that was fashioned by imperial powers.

Actually, the Filipino nationalist movement is an ongoing process and has passed through various phases. Originally, it represented the attempts of an educated native elite to wrest power from Spanish colonial authorities at both the political and ecclesiastical levels. This attempt was thwarted by the coming of the Americans, who imposed American sovereignty. During the American regime, it was the same native elite that agitated for independence. Nowadays, however, the nationalistic movement in the Philippines is manifested by an attempt by various sectors of the population to weld themselves progressively into a national community where members are characterized by increased consciousness of their nationality and loyalty to a larger political entity.

Indeed, the concept of pluralism need not be at odds with that of nationalism, which depends on loyalties to, and emotional support of, common national interests or endeavors. Nationalism may be slow to emerge in a strongly pluralistic or ethnically complex society, as has been the case in the Philippines: separate loyalties among ethnic groups, tribes, villages, and regions must be reconciled or transcended to allow fusion of loyalties in a common sense of national purpose. In spite of possible contradictory purposes the two concepts may imply, however, nationalism and pluralism need not offset each other. National unity ought to transcend cultural diversity without suppressing it; there ought not to be absolute divisiveness among Filipino groups. Yet at present, the Muslims cannot fully share a feeling of national unity with the Christians and other Filipinos—not so much because the two cultures and religions are so different as because the Filipino majority and the central government have discriminated against them, have mistreated them as if they were domestic colonials, have exploited the natural resources of their ancestral lands for the purposes of a capitalist economy or a few Manila capitalists, and have displaced them from these lands and forced thousands of them to drift as refugees or to migrate to new communities where they must rebuild their homes and lives without roots or ties.

All groups involved can still make efforts to nurture pluralism as a rich, beneficial, positive quality of Philippine society. First, Muslims ought not to consider themselves a minority group with underprivileged status; they ought not to identify always with their past condition as victims of discrimination. Unfortunately, too many of them seem to be taking advantage of a "favorable discrimination" status they have recently acquired.

Second, certain changes must take place in the hearts and minds of the non-Muslim majority if peace and unity are to return to the South. The Christians must abandon the attitude that their values, morals, and customs are superior to those of minority ethnic groups in the country. By developing greater tolerance toward other cultures, they might come to understand the values of those groups whom they are racially bonded with and whom they must live with as neighbors and fellow countrymen.

There are indications that a subtle shift in attitude—a "change of heart"—is already taking place and that the majority are close to accepting the cultural pluralism that is, whether they realize it or not, part of their own heritage.

For example, some non-Muslim Filipinos, especially those in Manila, are dismayed by news about the senseless killing of innocent Muslims. And the *moro-moro* syndrome, or mockery of the old stereotyped image of the Muslim Moro, is much less prevalent now among the Christians than it was a few generations ago. Many factors have contributed to this improved image of Muslims, including greater exposure of Filipinos to non-Filipino Muslims abroad. For example, there are about 120 thousand Filipino technicians and skilled workers in Saudi Arabia alone; and again that many in other parts of the Arab and Islamic world. Often while abroad, these Filipinos develop a more sophisticated outlook generally, and their new view of foreign Muslims tends to change their view of the Muslims in their own country when they return home.

* * *

FINALLY, THE GOVERNMENT must encourage acceptance
of cultural diversity in the Philippines. If, indeed, a true
change of heart is beginning to spread among the majority,
then the government should follow this example. The government must realize that Muslims cannot share in a national
identity unless the government itself takes the lead with its
voice of policymaking to support this new sentiment of tolerance.

The government must commit itself to making not only substantial concrete efforts—economic development programs,
executive orders, written agreements, and legislative or other
measurable steps toward granting autonomy—but some less
tangible efforts as well. This means changes in the general
attitude and policies of the administration, which can be
conveyed through specific commitments: to refrain from trying to assimilate the Muslims to cultural traditions not their
own; to refrain from catering to the army—indeed, to prohibit army abuses of innocent Muslims; to prohibit practices,
policies, or legislation that discriminate against Muslims or
other minority groups; to thwart any group's attempts to
displace Muslims or other minority groups from their territories; and to refrain from catering to self-serving traditional
Muslim "oligarchs" who would entrap their own people
in a "feudalistic" socioeconomic structure. The government
might also consider establishing a more liberal national educational system that would not promote nationalism to such
a degree that it would disparage pluralism (in its positive
sense of flavorful unity). Further, the government must commit itself to allowing Muslim communities to live and work
unhindered, to permitting them to preserve their faith, cultural heritage, and ethical and legal codes that govern most
aspects of their lives.

If Filipinos will acknowledge the advantages of pluralism,
if they will accept rather than reject it, then the various cultural groups can share in a common loyalty to the national
community while proudly retaining their distinctiveness. A
synthesized culture of this whole community could then emerge,

enriched by the diverse elements that compose it. Alternatively, if pluralism is not encouraged but increasingly resented, then the hatred and skirmishing might fester and break into a mass hysteria approaching genocide against one or more minority groups. Many Filipinos, as well as all countries worldwide, would furiously condemn genocide; and if Muslims were victims, then powerful or influential Muslim states would inevitably intervene.

* * *

TO PROTECT THEMSELVES from possible political changes or future whims of the government that could cripple their progress, Muslim Filipinos are now trying to improve their economic status and education. They feel an urgent need to compensate for lost time, for their having been slowly prepared to enter the Philippine business, professional, and academic milieus. They are interacting with other cultural groups, especially the Christians, within these milieus. They are earnestly cooperating with the government in reform programs designed to help them. Many MNLF members have returned to the jurisdiction of the law and have deferred to the government and military authorities: former MNLF commanders have found positions in government administration, and many of their followers have joined the regular army. These changes all show that Muslims can interrelate admirably with the government and the whole nation if not discriminated against and if assured that their cherished faith is not threatened.

As important as the Muslims' efforts to better their economic status and education and to interrelate with all Filipinos are their efforts to validate and preserve their cultural and religious identity. Opportunities to expand their knowledge about Islam are now available, including government-sponsored educational programs. Although increasingly exposed to Western and modern influences in their daily work, the Muslims have kept sight of their Islamic duties and ideals. And in spite of the tragedies associated with the armed conflict in the South, this conflict has served to prove their willingness to sacrifice their lives and so has served to increase their self-awareness as Muslims, as contributing members of a Muslim community.

With a firm knowledge of their heritage and present place in the religious community—and if neither this heritage nor this identity is threatened by the government or other groups —the Muslims will be free to contribute to the cultural and social needs of the larger community that is the Philippine nation. They will be in a position not only to better their own conditions but also to help improve the conditions of all Filipino citizens who are oppressed and to work toward peace and unity in the country.

The well-being and progress of the Muslim community ultimately depends on that of the whole national community. If the nation is in economic disorder, and if discrimination and social injustices against any Filipino groups continue unchecked, then the Muslims cannot expect much improvement in their own conditions. Whereas there is exploitation of Muslims by other Muslims—the self-serving politicians and "oligarchs," for example—as well as by Christians, there is also exploitation of Christians by other Christians throughout the country. There are many non-Muslim *barrios* and rural towns in other areas that are as poor as those in Muslim areas. And the army clashes not only with armed Muslims but also with outlaws, Communists, and other armed bands.

Meanwhile, sporadic fighting continues in the South and elsewhere. The sooner the government grants meaningful autonomy to the Muslims, returns most of the Muslim refugees to their former farms, and curbs army abuses, the sooner will peace and unity return to a nation that has seen so much suffering, bloodshed, and death.

APPENDIXES
* * *

APPENDIX ONE

MUSLIM LEADERS' CONSENSUS OF UNITY
In the Name of God, Most Great, Most Beneficent, Most Merciful

Faced by threats to the existence of the Islamic community in the Philippines on account of past and recent events, as a consensus of unity, after due deliberation, we hereby issue this communique stating:

We are all conscious and deeply concerned about our people's Islamic rights and obligations as Muslims and as citizens, and aware of the faithful trust of our people to work for their welfare and protect their rights from all forms of transgression;

That in order to facilitate this obligation we hereby unite as one body, setting aside all our personal and political differences in the past and in the present with an end to fight the enemies of our Muslim community;

That we have taken cognizance of past events which have befallen the Muslims in the Philippines, e.g., the Jabidah massacre, the disturbance of Muslim villages before resulting to the loss of lives and properties, the current series of killings, assault, and mutilations of Muslims, the desecration of their dead and the burning of their mosques and houses in Cotabato and Lanao del Sur, not to mention the perennial discrimination against Muslims in many levels of the national life as well as the misrepresentation or distortion of their true image as a historic people;

That unprovoked aggressions against Muslims, such as the merciless massacre of sixty-one Muslim men, women and children in a place of worship in the Manili mosque in Carmen, Cotabato, by "Ilaga" mercenaries who commit crimes of this magnitude with impunity, points out the fact that the Muslims are not getting the full measure of protection to which they are entitled under the laws of the land;

That all these barbaric and inhuman atrocities against the Muslims, like the cutting off the ears of Muslim dead, etc., is in violation of the Laws of God, of the Constitution and existing laws and is a serious and actual threat to the religious freedom of our people as well as an affront to the conscience and to the Universal Declaration of Human Rights of the United Nations;

That judging from the military capacity of the "Ilaga" marauders, as evidences are on hand, there is a strong reason to believe, of connivance with, or support by, certain sectors of the armed forces and local Christian politicians;

That this pattern of aggression and criminal actions in Muslim areas, unless immediately stopped by the government, adds to the belief that there is, indeed, a design to disperse and eliminate the Muslim community;

That in the case of the evacuees, the continued failure of the government to bring them back to their places of origin, compensate them for their losses unlike the immediate rehabilitation and replacement of houses in Ora Este and Ora Centro in Bantay, Ilocos Sur, and provide them protection, progressively erodes the confidence of the Muslims in the sincerity of the government to enforce their rights, protect their lives and their properties;

That in view of the foregoing facts and premises, we urge the government to accept our proposals to ensure lasting peace in the country and make the government forces protect the lives of not only the Christians but also the Muslims;

WE, THEREFORE, urge all the people behind the "Ilaga" mercenaries to desist from continuing their evil designs against the Muslims, for we know who they are and we know they can stop what they have started; unless they so desist, there shall be serious repercussions in the national life of this nation.

That we urge the Catholic hierarchy and other Christian groups to exercise their moral and spiritual leadership to appeal to their co-religionists to respect Islam and the Muslims as the basis for peace and harmony.

We appeal to all progressive and well-meaning Christians to exert their efforts in bringing about unity in order to prevent the disintegration of the nation;

Finally, if the government shall fail or refuse to perform its fundamental duty to give equal protection to all citizens, whether Muslim or Christian, if it fails to stop the criminal depredations in Muslim areas which are brazenly and openly committed with the very presence of the military and if we shall not get justice for our people thru peaceful and legal means—we hereby pledge today before God, that despite our present personal and political positions, we shall do our utmost to preserve our community and land. Toward this end, we are willing and ready to sacrifice our worldly possessions and even our lives as our forebears have done before us in defense of freedom and Islam.

Manila, July 15, 1971

SIGNATORIES:

(Sgd.) Senator Mamintal A. Tamano
President, Muslim Lawyers
League of the Philippines

(Sgd.) Rep. Salipada K. Pendatun
President, Muslim Association
of the Philippines

(Sgd.) Rep. Ali Dimaporo
President, Supreme Council for
Islamic Affairs of the Philippines

(Sgd.) Delegate Domocao Alonto
Director General
Anzar El-Islam

(Sgd.) Sultan Rashid Lucman
Chairman, Union of Islamic
Forces of the Philippines

(Sgd.) Atty. Sandiale Sambolawan
Constitutional Delegate
Cotabato City

(Sgd.) Rep. Macacana Dimaporo
Lanao del Sur

(Sgd.) Atty. Benjamin Abubakar
Former Governor
Jolo, Sulu

(Sgd.) Kasan Marohombzar
Vice Governor
Lanao del Sur

(Sgd.) Pullong Arpa
Former Ambassador
Jolo, Sulu

(Sgd.) Dean Cesar Adib Majul
    College of Arts & Sciences
    U.P., Diliman, Quezon City

(Sgd.) Datu Udtog Matalam, Jr.
    Pikit, Cotabato

(Sgd.) Former Gov. Hadji Arsad Sali
    Jolo, Sulu

(Sgd.) Mus Izquierdo
    Provincial Board Member
    Jolo, Sulu

(Sgd.) Atty. Midpantao Adil
    Constitutional Delegate
    Pagalungan, Cotabato

(Sgd.) Delegate M. Guro
    Lanao del Sur

(Sgd.) Lininding Pangandaman
    Constitutional Delegate
    Lanao del Sur

(Sgd.) Atty. Michael Mastura
    Constitutional Delegate
    Cotabato City

(Sgd.) Nur Misuari
    University of the Philippines

(Sgd.) Atty. M. Y. Abbas, Jr.
    Chairman, Muslim Youth
    National Assembly

(Sgd.) Engr. Farouk Carpizo
    Secretary-General, National
    Coordination Council for Islamic
    Affairs, Inc.

(Sgd.) Atty. Musib Buat
    Nurul Islam
    Cotabato

(Sgd.) Ustadz Kunug Pumbaya
    Imam, Manila Mosque

(Sgd.) Atty. Abraham Rasul
    Former CNI Commissioner
    Jolo, Sulu

(Sgd.) Atty. Madki Alonto
    Former Governor
    Lanao del Sur

(Sgd.) Aminkadra Abubakar
    Mayor, Jolo, Sulu

(Sgd.) Manaros Boransing
    Professor, Mindanao State
    University

(Sgd.) Ustadz Calbi Tupay
    Basilan City

(Sgd.) Kalingalan Kaluang
    Jolo, Sulu

(Sgd.) Capt. Hassan Bagis
    Jolo, Sulu

By the Muslim Leaders in the Philippines

(Taken from *The Manila Times*, Wednesday, July 21, 1971)

APPENDIX TWO

MANIFESTO ON THE ESTABLISHMENT
OF THE BANGSAMORO REPUBLIK

WE, the oppressed Bangsamoro people, Wishing to free ourselves from the terror, oppression and tyranny of Filipino colonialism which has caused us untold suffering and misery by criminally usurping our land, by threatening Islam through [wholesale] destruction and desecration of its places of worship and its Holy Book, and murdering our innocent brothers, sisters and old folks in a genocidal campaign of terrifying magnitude;

ASPIRING to have the sole prerogative of defining and chartering our own national destiny in accordance with our own free will in order to ensure our future and that of our children;

Having evolved an appropriate form of ideology with which the unity of our people has been firmly established and their national identity and character strengthened;

HAVING established the Moro National Liberation Front and its military arm, the Bangsamoro Army, as our principal instrument for achieving our primary goals and objectives with the unanimous support of the great masses of our people; and finally,

BEING now in firm control of a great portion of our national homeland through the successive and smashing victories of our Bangsamoro Army in battle against the armed forces of the Philippines and the Marcos dictatorship, hereby declare:

—THAT, henceforth, the Bangsamoro people and Revolution, having established their Bangsamoro Republik, are disbonding all their political, economic, and other bonds with the oppressive government of the Philippines under the dictatorial regime of President Ferdinand Marcos to secure a free and independent state for the Bangsamoro people;

—THAT we believe armed struggle is the only means by which we could achieve the complete freedom and independence of our people, since Marcos and his government will never dismantle the edifice of Philippine colonial rule in our homeland of their own accord;

—THAT our people and Revolution, upholding the principle of self-determination, support the right of all peoples of all nations in their legitimate and just struggle for national survival, freedom, and independence;

—THAT the Bangsamoro people and Revolution shall in the interest of truth guarantee the freedom of the press;

—THAT in order to accelerate the economic progress of our war-ravaged Bangsamoro homeland, our people and Revolution shall encourage foreign investment under terms and conditions beneficial to our people and the investors. Accordingly, those foreign investors in the Bangsamoro homeland who may decide to continue their economic activities under the revolutionary regime shall be welcomed;

—THAT the Bangsamoro people and Revolution are committed to the principle that they are a part of the Islamic World as well as of the Third World and of the oppressed colonized humanity everywhere in the world;

—THAT the Moro National Liberation Front and its military arm, the Bangsamoro Army, shall not agree to any form of settlement or accord short of achieving total freedom and independence for our oppressed Bangsamoro people;

—THAT the revolution of the Bangsamoro people is a revolution with a social conscience. As such they are committed to the principle of establishing a democratic system of government which shall never allow nor tolerate any form of exploitation and oppression of any human being by another or of one nation by another;

—THAT those Filipinos who may wish to remain in the Bangsamoro national homeland even after independence shall be welcomed and entitled to equal rights and protection with all other citizens of the Bangsamoro Republik, provided that they formally renounce their Filipino citizenship and wholeheartedly accept Bangsamoro citizenship, their property rights shall be fully respected and the exercise of their political, cultural and religious rights shall be guaranteed;

—THAT the Bangsamoro people and Revolution are committed to the preservation and growth of Islamic culture among our people without prejudice to the development and growth of other religious and indigenous cultures in our homeland;

—THAT our people and Revolution recognize and adhere to the charter of the United Nations and the Universal Declaration of Human Rights. And, in addition, they shall respect and adhere to all laws and conventions binding upon the nations of the world;

—THAT the Bangsamoro people and Revolution are committed to the preservation and enhancement of world peace through mutual cooperation among nations and common progress of the peoples of the world. Accordingly, they are committed to the principle of mutual respect and friendship among nations irrespective of their ideological and religious creed;

THEREFORE, we hereby appeal to the conscience [of] all men everywhere and the sympathy of all nations of the world to help accelerate the pace of our Revolution by formally and unequivocally recognizing and supporting our people's legitimate right to obtain their national freedom and independence. Such recognition and support must be concretized by accepting the Bangsamoro Republik as one of the members of the family of independent and sovereign nations in the world and giving official recognition to the Moro National Liberation Front.

DONE in the Bangsamoro homeland, this 18th day of March 1974.

Nur Misuari, *Chairman, Central Committee*
Moro National Liberation Front

(Taken from *Mahardika*, Vol. IX, No. 1, 1982)

APPENDIX THREE

In the Name of God, the Omnipotent, the Merciful

AGREEMENT BETWEEN THE GOVERNMENT OF THE
REPUBLIC OF THE PHILIPPINES AND THE MORO
NATIONAL LIBERATION FRONT WITH THE
PARTICIPATION OF THE QUADRIPARTITE
MINISTERIAL COMMISSION MEMBERS OF THE ISLAMIC
CONFERENCE AND THE SECRETARY GENERAL OF
THE ISLAMIC CONFERENCE

In accordance with Resolution No. 4 Para. 5 adopted by the
Council of Ministers of the Islamic Conference in its Fourth
Session held in Benghazi, Libyan Arab Republic during the
month of Safar 1393 H. corresponding to March 1973, calling
for the formation of the Quadripartite Ministerial Commission
representing the Libyan Arab Republic, the Kingdom of Saudi
Arabia, the Republic of Senegal and the Republic of Somalia, to
enter into discussions with the Government of the Republic of
the Philippines concerning the situation of the Muslims in the
South of the Philippines.

And in accordance with Resolution No. (18) adopted by the
Islamic Conference held in Kuala Lumpur, Malaysia in Jumada
Alakhir 1393 H. corresponding to June 1974 A.D. which
recommends the searching for a just and peaceful political solution to the problem of the Muslims in the South of the Philippines through the negotiations.

And in accordance with Resolution No. 12/7/S adopted by the
Islamic Conference held in Istambul in Jumada El-Ula 1396 H.
corresponding to May 1976 A.D. empowering the Quadripartite Ministerial Commission and the Secretary General of the
Islamic Conference to take the necessary steps for the resumption of negotiations.

And following the task undertaken by the Quadripartite Ministerial Commission and the Secretary General of the Islamic
Conference and the discussions held with H.E. President Marcos, President of the Republic of the Philippines.

And in realization of the contents of Para. (6) of the Joint
Communique issued in Tripoli on the 25th Zulgeda 1396 H.

corresponding to 17th November 1976 A.D. following the official visit paid by the delegation of the Government of the Philippines headed by the First Lady of the Philippines Mrs. IMELDA ROMUALDEZ MARCOS to the Libyan Arab Republic and which calls for the resumption of negotiations between the two parties concerned in Tripoli on the 15th of December 1976 A.D.

Negotiations were held in the City of Tripoli during the period between 24th Zulhija 1396 H. to second of Moharram 1397 H. corresponding to the period from 15th to 23rd December 1976 A.D. at the Ministry of Foreign Affairs presided over by Dr. Ali Abdussalam Treki, Minister of State for Foreign Affairs of the Libyan Arab Republic, and comprising the Delegations of:

1. Government of the Republic of the Philippines, led by Honorable Carmelo Z. Barbero, Undersecretary of National Defense for Civilian Relations.
2. Moro National Liberation Front, led by Mr. Nur Misuari, Chief of the Front.

And with the participation of the representatives of the Quadripartite Ministerial Commission:

The Libyan Arab Republic—Dr. Ali Abdussalam Treki, Minister of State for Foreign Affairs.

The Kingdom of Saudi Arabia—H.E. Salah Abdalla El-Fadl, Ambassador of the Kingdom of Saudi Arabia, Libyan Arab Republic.

The Republic of Senegal—Mr. Abubakar Othman Si, Representative of the Republic of Senegal and Charge d'Affairs of Senegal in Cairo.

Democratic Republic of Somalia—H.E. Bazi Mohamed Sufi, Ambassador of the Democratic Republic of Somalia, Libyan Arab Republic.

With the aid of H.E. Dr. Ahmed Karim Gai, Secretary General of the Islamic Conference, and a delegation from the Secretariat General of the Conference composed of Mr. Qasim Zuheri, Assistant Secretary General, and Mr. Aref Ben Musa, Director of the Political Department.

During these negotiations, which were marked by a spirit of conciliation and understanding, it has been agreed on the following:

First: The establishment of Autonomy in the Southern Philippines within the realm of the sovereignty and territorial integrity of the Republic of the Philippines.

Second: The areas of autonomy for the Muslims in the Southern Philippines shall comprise the following:

1. Basilan
2. Sulu
3. Tawi-Tawi
4. Zamboanga del Sur
5. Zamboanga del Norte
6. North Cotabato
7. Maguindanao
8. Sultan Kudarat
9. Lanao del Norte
10. Lanao del Sur
11. Davao del Sur
12. South Cotabato
13. Palawan
14. All the cities and villages situated in the above mentioned areas.

Third:

1. Foreign policy shall be of the competence of the Central Government of the Philippines.
2. The National Defense Affairs shall be the concern of the Central Authority provided that the arrangements for the joining of the forces of the Moro National Liberation Front with the Philippines Armed Forces be discussed later.
3. In the areas of the autonomy, the Muslims shall have the right to set up their own Courts which implement the Islamic Shari'a laws. The Muslims shall be represented in all Courts including the Supreme Court. The representation of the Muslims in the Supreme Court shall be upon the recommendation from the authorities of the Autonomy and the Supreme Court. Decrees will be issued by the President of the Republic for their appointments

taking into consideration all necessary qualifications of the candidates.

4. Authorities in the autonomy in the South of the Philippines shall have the right to set up schools, colleges, and universities, provided that matters pertaining to the relationship between these educational and scientific organs and the general education system in the State shall be subject of discussion later on.

5. The Muslims shall have their own administrative system in compliance with the objectives of the autonomy and its institutions. The relationship between this administrative system and the Central administrative system to be discussed later.

6. The authorities of the autonomy in the South of the Philippines shall have their own economic and financial system. The relationship between this system and the Central economic and financial system of the State shall be discussed later.

7. The authorities of the autonomy in the South of the Philippines shall enjoy the right of representation and participation in the Central Government and in all other organs of the State. The number of representatives and ways of participation shall be fixed later.

8. Special Regional Security Forces are to be set up in the autonomous areas for the Muslims in the Southern Philippines. The relationship between these forces and the central security forces shall be fixed later.

9. A Legislative Assembly and an Executive Council shall be formed in the areas of the Autonomy for the Muslims. The setting up of the Legislative Assembly shall be constituted through a direct election, and the formation of the Executive Council shall take place through appointments by the Legislative Assembly. A decree for their formation shall be enacted by the President of the Republic respectively. The number of members of each assembly shall be determined later on.

10. Mines and mineral resources fall within the competence of the Central Government, and a reasonable percentage deriving from the revenues of the mines and minerals

[shall] be used for the benefit of the areas of the autonomy.

11. A mixed Committee shall be composed of representatives of the Central Government of the Republic of the Philippines and representatives of the Moro National Liberation Front. The mixed Committee shall meet in Tripoli during the period from the Fifth of February to a date not later than the *Third of March 1977*. The task of said Committee shall be charged to study in detail the points left for discussion in order to reach a solution thereof in conformity with the provisions of this agreement.

12. Cease-fire shall be declared immediately after the signature of this agreement, provided that its coming into effect [is by] the 20th of January 1977. A Joint Committee shall be composed of the two parties with the help of the Organization of the Islamic Conference represented by the Quadripartite Ministerial Commission to supervise the implementation of the cease-fire. The said Joint Committee shall also be charged with supervising the following:

   a. A complete amnesty in the areas of the autonomy and the renunciation of all legal claims and codes resulting from events which took place in the South of the Philippines.

   b. The release of all the political prisoners who had relations with the events in the South of the Philippines.

   c. The return of all refugees who have abandoned their areas in the South of the Philippines.

   d. To guarantee the freedom of movements and meetings.

13. A joint meeting [shall] be held in Jeddah during the first week of the month of March 1977 to initial what has been concluded by the Committee referred to in Para. 11.

14. The final agreement concerning the setting up of the autonomy referred to in the first and second paragraphs shall be signed in the City of Manila, Republic of the Philippines, between the Government of the Philippines and Moro National Liberation Front, and the Islamic Conference represented by the Quadripartite Ministerial

Commission and the Secretary General of the Organization of Islamic Conference.

15. Immediately after the signature of the Agreement in
    Manila, a Provisional Government shall be established
    in the areas of the autonomy to be appointed by the
    President of the Philippines; and be charged with the
    task of preparing for the elections of the Legislative
    Assembly in the territories of the Autonomy; and admin-
    ister the areas in accordance with the provisions of this
    agreement until a Government is formed by the elected
    Legislative Assembly.

16. The government of the Philippines shall take all neces-
    sary constitutional processes for the implementation of
    the entire Agreement.

Fourth: This Agreement shall come into force with effect
from the date of its signature.

Done in the City of Tripoli on 2nd Muharram 1397 H.
corresponding to 23rd December 1976 A.D. in three original
copies in Arabic, English, French languages, all equal in legal
power.

For the Government of the   *For the Moro National*
Republic of the Philippines: *Liberation Front:*

Hon. Carmelo Z. Barbero   Mr. Nur Misuari
Undersecretary of National   *Chairman of the Front*
Defense for Civilian
Relations

Dr. Ali Abdussalam Treki   Dr. Ahmed Karim Gai
Minister of State for Foreign   *Secretary General of the*
Affairs, Libyan Arab Republic   *Organization of the Islamic*
and Chairman of the   *Conference*
Negotiations

APPENDIX FOUR

MALACANANG
MANILA
PROCLAMATION NO. 1628
DECLARING AUTONOMY IN
SOUTHERN PHILIPPINES

WHEREAS, in an agreement executed on December 23, 1976 between the Republic of the Philippines and the Moro National Liberation Front with the participation of representatives of the Conference and with the assistance of the Secretary General of the Islamic Conference, it was agreed that within the realm of the sovereignty and territorial integrity of the Republic of the Philippines, autonomy shall be declared in 13 provinces of Southern Philippines;

WHEREAS, in subsequent negotiations held from February 9, 1977 to March 3, 1977, also at Tripoli, Libya, the parties were unable to agree on certain vital aspects of the autonomy to be established in Southern Philippines;

WHEREAS, the First Lady Imelda Romualdez Marcos visited Libya from March 12-22, 1977 and on the occasion of said visit discussed with Col. M. Khaddafy, the leader of the Great First of September Revolution of the People's Socialist Libyan Arab Jemeheriya, the problem in Southern Philippines, in light of an impasse in the negotiations held from February 9, 1977 to March 3, 1977;

WHEREAS, in the course of said discussions, Col. M. Khaddafy proposed to break the impasse in the aforementioned negotiations with the declaration by President Ferdinand E. Marcos of autonomy for the thirteen (13) provinces mentioned in the Tripoli Agreement of December 23, 1976 within the realm of the sovereignty and territorial integrity of the Republic of the Philippines, the organization of a provisional government for such areas of autonomy, in which provisional government the concerned parties of the Moro National Liberation Front and the inhabitants of the areas of autonomy shall take part and the holding of a referendum by the provisional government concerning the manner in which the inhabitants within the areas of autonomy may wish to organize themselves administratively in accordance with the Constitution of the Philippines;

WHEREAS, on the following day, March 19, 1977, President Ferdinand E. Marcos informed Col. Muammar Al Ghaddafi of his approval of the above proposals;

WHEREAS, immediately after the receipt of the telegram of President Ferdinand E. Marcos dated March 19, 1977, Col. Muammar Al Ghaddafi informed President Ferdinand E. Marcos by telegram of the approval of the agreed formula by the Members of the Quadripartite Ministerial Committee of the Islamic Conference, the current President of the Islamic Conference and the Islamic States supporting the endeavours of the People's Socialist Libyan Arab Jemeheriya and requesting that the same be implemented at the earliest possible time;

NOW, THEREFORE, I, FERDINAND E. MARCOS, President of the Philippines, by virtue of the powers vested in me by the Constitution, do hereby declare autonomy in Southern Philippines to be composed of the provinces of Basilan, Sulu, Tawi-Tawi, Zamboanga del Norte, Zamboanga del Sur in Region 9, Lanao del Norte, Lanao del Sur, Maguindanao, North Cotabato, Sultan Kudarat in Region 12, Palawan in Region 4, and Davao del Sur and South Cotabato in Region 11.

Prior to the establishment of the Regional Legislative Assembly and the Executive Council as envisioned in the Tripoli Agreement dated December 23, 1976, there is hereby created a Provisional Regional Government in the above-mentioned areas to be composed of seven (7) members appointed by the President, two (2) of whom shall be from the Moro National Liberation Front and one (1) member to be recommended by other liberation fronts in the provinces concerned. Its main functions, powers and responsibilities are as follows:

1. To prepare for the referendum in the said areas;
2. To prepare for the election of the regional legislative assembly in the said areas;
3. To administer said areas in accordance with the existing laws and policies governing the activities presently being undertaken by the local government units therein; and

4. To exercise such other powers as the President of the
   Philippines may direct.

The results of the referendum of April 17, 1977 shall determine the manner in which the inhabitants of the areas of
autonomy may wish to reorganize themselves administratively
in accordance with the Constitution of the Philippines and the
formula proposed by Col. Muammar Al Ghaddafi, the leader
of the Great First of September Revolution of the People's
Socialist Libyan Arab Jemeheriya.

IN WITNESS WHEREOF, I have hereunto set my hand
and caused the seal of the Republic of the Philippines to be
affixed.

Done in the City of Manila, this 25th day of March, in the
year of Our Lord, nineteen hundred and seventy-seven.

(Sgd.) Ferdinand E. Marcos
President of the Republic of the Philippines

by the President:
(Sgd.) Juan C. Tuvera
Presidential Assistant

APPENDIX FIVE

PRESS STATEMENT OF SECRETARY
CARLOS P. ROMULO ON MAY 1, 1977

On 21 April, an official panel headed by the Secretary of Foreign Affairs began conversations in Manila with members of the Quadripartite Ministerial Committee of the Islamic Conference on the final details of the settlement of the problem in Southern Philippines.

The delegation was accorded the full courtesy and hospitality of the Philippine Government, as befits its members who represent friendly Islamic states interested in helping the Republic of the Philippines find a just and lasting solution to the problem which involves rebels of the Moro National Liberation Front.

We sought in these conversations full application of the understanding reached in Tripoli in December between representatives of the Philippine Government and representatives of the MNLF, and of the understanding contained in an exchange of cables between Col. Moammer Ghaddafi, leader of the Great September Revolution of the Socialist People's Libyan Arab Jamahiriya and President Marcos on March 18 and 19 respectively.

We regret to announce that the MNLF chose to introduce during these conversations unacceptable demands that violate the Constitution of the Republic of the Philippines, negate the views of inhabitants of Southern Philippines who are not members of the MNLF, and set aside previous understandings reached between representatives of the Philippine Government and those of the MNLF, as well as between President Marcos and President Ghaddafi.

We also regret to announce that on account of this, our conversations had to adjourn at the initiative of the Quadripartite Committee without a final settlement having been reached.

It is our hope that this impasse is temporary and that the conversations will soon be resumed.

The Republic of the Philippines entered into two documents in an effort to arrive at a just and lasting solution to the peace and order problem in her Southern regions. These documents are: one, The Tripoli Agreement of 23 December 1976, an understanding with representatives of the Moro National Liberation Front, in their capacity as Filipino nationals; two, the Ghaddafi-Marcos exchange of cables which constituted an agreement between the two heads of state on steps leading to a settlement with the MNLF.

Under these cables, autonomy was to be declared by the President in 13 provinces in Southern Philippines, a provisional government organized by decision of the President, in which the MNLF would participate, and finally, a referendum would be held in the 13 provinces to ascertain the people's will on administrative arrangements.

On 25 March 1977, the President declared autonomy in all 13 provinces concerned and organized the provisional government, offering 15 seats to the MNLF, as against the 14 seats for the other non-MNLF sectors of the 13 provinces.

The provisional government, subsequently meeting in Zamboanga, called for the immediate holding of a referendum by formal resolution, later on adopting questions proposed by the inhabitants of the areas of autonomy, based on specific proposals advanced by the MNLF.

On April 17, a referendum was held in the areas of autonomy. The results rejected the proposal to merge the 13 areas of autonomy into one region and also the proposed MNLF control of the areas of autonomy. Diplomatic observers from 20 countries as well as foreign correspondents were on hand to closely watch and supervise the proceedings, and they were unanimous in their view that the referendum was free, peaceful, untrammelled and orderly, and that it was an accurate expression of the people's will. Even representatives of the MNLF agreed that this was so.

The MNLF, the Quadripartite Ministerial Committee of the Islamic Conference and the Secretary-General of the Islamic Conference knew of the call to the referendum and not only approved of it, but participated in the decision to include it in the Tripoli Agreement, specifically Article 16 thereof, which refers to a faithful compliance with constitutional processes of the Republic of the Philippines in the solution of the

Mindanao problem. With respect to the Ghaddafi-Marcos exchange of cables, this was fully recognized by the Islamic Conference, the Quadripartite Ministerial Committee and the Chairman of the Central Committee of the MNLF. Their participation in the decision to hold the referendum is further reflected in the fact that questions were suggested by them, questions which formed part of those that were finally asked at the referendum.

Unfortunately they changed their position and questioned the holding of the referendum which they had until then supported, a few days before it was to be held, when it was too late to either cancel or postpone it.

Now, the MNLF and the members of the Quadripartite Committee seek to nullify the results of the referendum first, by setting aside the Ghaddafi-Marcos exchange of cables, which both the MNLF and the Islamic Conference had earlier recognized, and by modifying the Tripoli document of 23 December 1976.

They now contend that the provisional government can be organized only upon the prior approval of the Central Committee of the MNLF, a provision that neither exists in any of the two documents referred to herein, nor was discussed at any time during the negotiations.

They also now demand full control by the foreign-based Central Committee of the MNLF of the provisional government, through the appointment of 11 members, seven of whom are to be drawn from the MNLF, and the four others (two Muslim and two non-Muslim) to be chosen also by the MNLF. Under this proposal of full MNLF control, in the final government to be set up for the 13 provinces, there is to be one legislative assembly, to be composed of 26 elective members and five appointed members, three of the latter to be recommended by the MNLF. Of the 26 elective members, two Muslims each will come from the Provinces of Sulu, Tawi-Tawi, Basilan, Lanao del Sur, Lanao Norte, Maguindanao, Sultan Kudurat, and Zamboanga del Sur. One Muslim and one non-Muslim will each come from North Cotabato, Zamboanga Norte, Davao Sur, South Cotabato and Palawan. There is also to be one executive council for the 13 provinces, to be composed of 11 members, seven of whom shall come from the MNLF and the 4 others (two Muslims and two non-Muslims) to be chosen by the MNLF.

The MNLF is to have a separate military unit representing 25 percent of the strength of the Armed Forces of the Philippines, estimated by them at 15,000 men to be paid and equipped by the Philippine Government, but to be under the command of the MNLF, and under no circumstance to be employed by the AFP either within or outside the area of autonomy.

The provisional government controlled by the foreign-based Central Committee of the MNLF, is to have a transition period of six years, with full powers to change governors and mayors and other officers of the government as well as employees thus giving the MNLF unlimited power to change elective and appointive officials within the 13 provinces.

The MNLF further wants that the finances of the areas of autonomy be exempt from the standard auditing procedures and audited only by an appointee of the MNLF.

We regard these demands of the MNLF as violative of the Constitution of the Republic of the Philippines, of the resounding will by the people of the 13 provinces expressed at the 17 April referendum, of the Tripoli document, and the Ghaddafi-Marcos exchange of cables, which provide that any settlement shall not violate the "sovereignty and territorial integrity" of the Republic of the Philippines.

The record of our effort to find a just and lasting settlement of the Mindanao problem has not been wanting of conciliation and accommodation. President Marcos embarked on this effort first by adopting a nonmilitary approach to the problem. He authorized the largest socio-economic reconstruction program ever attempted by the government in Mindanao, created new provinces under Muslim officials, appointed qualified Muslims to high positions in the judiciary and other high positions of leadership in the country. He also granted amnesty to those who had engaged in rebellion, going so far as to allow for integration into the armed forces of those who are qualified and desire to be so integrated. Finally, President Marcos granted autonomy and organized a provisional government in the 13 provinces, with [the] majority of the officers thereof coming from the MNLF.

The MNLF insistence on demands that are repugnant to our Constitution as well as to the untrammelled will of our people has set back our effort to arrive at a just and lasting peaceful settlement of our problem in Mindanao. But we are prepared to go to any length to explore every possible avenue that offers an opportunity for mutual understanding and settlement. We remain ever hopeful that we are joined in this by all those who have until now taken part in our effort to find peace, justice and brotherhood for all our people in Mindanao, and that the final solution having been shown to be still fraught with problems that we must jointly resolve, all parties would contribute their utmost to the work of finalizing the details of that settlement.

APPENDIX SIX

CULTURAL GENOCIDE IN THE PHILIPPINES

(Speech delivered by Nur Misuari, Chairman, Central Committee of the Moro National Liberation Front, before the International Congress on Cultural Imperialism sponsored by the Lelio Basso Peace Foundation and held at the Palais des Nations, Algiers, Algeria, from 11 to 15 October 1977.)

To begin with, allow me to convey the fraternal greetings of our people and the Central Committee of the Moro National Liberation Front to this International Congress on Cultural Imperialism and to the Lelio Basso Peace Foundation for the invitation to participate in this historic meeting of anti-imperialist forces in the world. Our boundless thanks go to the Algerian People and Government for their generous and brotherly welcome and for their firm support behind the just cause of our people.

Comrades in the cause of world peace and freedom: Today, as we listen to each other and discuss vital problems of the world we live in, there in South Philippines, the home of 5.5 million Muslim and another million indigenous people, a new war is raging with all its force and fury.

The physical and spiritual existence or well-being of a Muslim nation is precariously at stake. The colonial government of President Marcos, supported by American imperialism, World Zionism, Japanese and Western monopoly capital, is engaged in a new round of war of genocide against our people.

A War of Genocide as a Reflection of a Colonial Order
This genocidal campaign against the Bangsa Moro nation is 9 years old, starting with the cold-blooded massacre of 68 Muslim youths in the historic island of Corregidor in March 1968. This is not to mention the earlier crimes of Filipino colonialism against our people. Up to these days, over one-hundred of our youths who, together with those executed in the Corregidor tragedy, were recruited clandestinely by the Special Forces of President Marcos for the abortive invasion of the State of Sabah, are still missing.

This incident was followed closely by the launching of the notorious Ilaga gang by the Armed Forces of the Philippines. The Philippine colonial government, exploiting the deep-rooted hatred of the colonial settlers towards our people, organized, trained and armed the Christian settlers in all parts of our homeland and caused them to commit all acts of depredation and savagery against our people, homeland and national culture.

In November 1972, barely two months following the unlawful imposition of Martial Law in the Philippines and the installation of the present dictatorial regime of President Marcos and his military collaborators, the Philippine colonial government finally declared war against our people. Since then South Philippines has been engulfed in a violent conflagration, which has wrought havoc and destruction on our people, as witness the death of about 50,000 innocent Muslim women, children and other civilians, the burning of 200,000 houses and over 500 mosques, several hundreds of Islamic schools and madrasas and vast plantation areas. Thirty-seven Muslim cities and municipalities, including the historic capital of the once powerful Islamic government of the Sultanate of Sulu, have been pulverized by cannons, bombs and napalm.

In addition, millions of our people have been uprooted from their homes and became refugees and are now exposed to famine, sickness and the like. This includes 92,000 Muslim refugees who have fled to Sabah, not to mention those affected by the latest military campaign of Marcos and his colonial armed forces.

What's more, as the colonial government of Marcos pursues its act of repression and extermination, it is certain to commit additional crimes against our people and humanity.

For this reason, I would like to ask your favor to focus more attention to this South Philippines problem and adopt this problem as part and parcel of the problems confronting the revolutionary world, the Third World and the peace-loving peoples of the world.

Already the Islamic World, which constitutes over 40 countries in Asia and Africa and represents nearly one-fourth of mankind, has defined its stand and is strongly in support of our people's just cause.

I would like to say that the problem that afflicts our people is very much a part of the problem that grips the world at large.

In truth, the war in South Philippines is a reflection and indeed a product of a colonial order. And the South Philippines problem is therefore organically linked with our global colonial reality.

The Muslim people and homeland have 500 years of Islamic culture and civilization. They were once free, sovereign and an independent nation. As a matter of fact, they were once one of the strongest powers in Southeast Asia. From early 16th century until the close of the 19th century and on till the end of the Second World War, they fought one of the longest and bitterest anti-colonial wars in history.

For 33 years they held Spanish colonialism at bay, not to speak of the sporadic intrusion of Portuguese, Dutch, British, French and German colonialism. And from the beginning of our present century, in the wake of the dissolution of Spanish colonialism in the Philippines, our people were once again locked in an anti-colonial or anti-imperialist war. This time, they found themselves face to face with a newly-emerging colonial government, namely the United States of America.

For more than four decades, until the outbreak of the last Pacific war, our people fought against this new colossus, followed by a few years of violent confrontation with Japanese imperialism during the four years (1942–1945) of Japanese interregnum in the Philippines and its extension to our people's homeland after the defeat of American imperialism early in the war.

As you can see, our people have never been lacking in vigilance, more so when it comes to the defence and protection of their national freedom and independence.

But you'll understand, what a great odds our people had to face after the end of the Second World War and the emergence of US imperialist hegemony in our part of the world.

The Advent of Filipino Colonialism in the Muslim
National Homeland

Taking advantage of the total confusion and trauma in the

aftermath of the war, the US imperialist government, in its decision to grant independence to the Filipino people, entered into a collusion with its Filipino puppets to arbitrarily place our people under Filipino colonial rule and domination.

This fateful incident occurred on July 4, 1946, some 30 years ago. Before that our people were never part of the Filipino nation. They were separate—free and sovereign. Even when the idea of unifying our people was broached for the first time in the 1930s by the US colonial government, our people vehemently opposed such a sinister scheme: witness the famous March 18, 1935 Manifesto of the Bangsa Moro people addressed to the US Congress and the US President.

It can be correctly said that the present war in South Philippines is or was once also true to all the colonized peoples of the world, be it in Africa, Latin America or Asia.

At the same time, as a reaction to such a regime of colonial exploitation, oppression and tyranny, the oppressed colonized people are inevitably dragged into a violent clash with their colonial ruler, thereby accelerating the development of the revolutionary process and the revolutionary consciousness of the oppressed colonized people and unleashing at a certain stage their revolutionary energy and dynamism.

Such is the case of the emergence of the Bangsa Moro Revolution led by the Moro National Liberation Front.

Muslim Protest Against Filipino Colonialism is Not New

Our people have certainly been protesting against such unjust colonial imposition from the very start. A series of armed rebellions have been staged by our people, the most famous being the Kamlen rebellion, the Tawan-Tawan rebellion, the Hajal Ooh rebellion, and the peaceful independence campaign of the late Sultan Ombra Amilbangsa of the Sultanate of Sulu.

But such struggles were all aborted for one reason or other, and most particularly on account of their limited ideological scope and relative isolation.

But the present Bangsa Moro Revolution led by the Moro National Liberation Front is the culmination of such anti-colonial and anti-imperialist experiences. And it came at a time when our internal colonial contradiction has reached its breaking point in view of the intensification of the colonial aggres-

sion in all its political, economic, social, religious and cultural
dimensions. Moreover, the Bangsa Moro Revolution has been
influenced by the revolutionary ferment in the world.

The Rise of the MNLF

The Philippine colonial government, particularly under President Marcos, has curtailed and suppressed our people's political freedom. They usurped our people's economic rights by
depriving them of their traditional sources of livelihood, specifically their ancestral land. Besides, they flouted the socio-
religious and cultural rights of our people by imposing a total-
itarian social order, which is embarked on the creation of a
so-called "New Society".

This conception of a new society is but a misnomer for a
more repressive colonial regime in South Philippines, which is
being used to justify the brutal suppression of our people's
Islamic and indigenous culture and supplanting them with the
Filipino colonial culture. This Filipino colonial culture is
fundamentally a reflection of Western Christian civilization—
inherited from Spanish and American colonialism.

The Philippine colonial regime is now engaged in a programme which calls for total and complete integration of the
so-called cultural minorities to which our people are classified.

In truth, this is a colonial scheme designed to complement
its campaign of genocide against the physical existence of our
people. In reality, therefore, this cultural scheme constitutes a
cultural genocide, intended to annihilate the spiritual and
cultural identity of our people.

It must be said that behind this cultural genocide is the
sinister colonial attempt to destroy our people's national identity, which is essentially founded on our cultural reality.

However, as the Philippine colonial government pursues its
criminal design, our people are all the more become alienated
from the cultural milieu and are driven to the other extreme of
the colonial spectrum.

This led to the appearance of a revolutionary consciousness
among our people and the rise of the Moro National Liberation Front.

The MNLF is the Vanguard of the Bangsa Moro Revolution

The Moro National Liberation Front, to be specific, came into being some years before the formal launching by Marcos of his anti-Muslim genocidal campaign. While the MNLF had been directly involved in the anti-Ilaga resistance, yet it did not surface formally until the colonial violence had become widespread following Marcos' declaration of war in November 1972. It stayed deliberately in the background while the masses of our people were putting up their own resistance against the colonial terror.

But once the MNLF was caught in the revolutionary storm, starting with the famous November 14, 1972 encounter in the historic island of Jolo, which was the bastion of our people's resistance during their 400 years of anti-colonial and anti-imperialist resistance, it rapidly became the rallying point of the Bangsa Moro Revolution.

Thus since this last 5½ years of intense fighting, interrupted only by the 9 months of ceasefire arranged by the Quadripartite Ministerial Commission and the Islamic Conference, the MNLF has assumed the role of the vanguard of the Bangsa Moro people and Revolution.

National Freedom and Independence: The MNLF's Initial Political Objective

And in keeping with the desire of the broad masses of our people, the MNLF adopted a political programme which called for the complete liberation of our people and national homeland from all forms and vestiges of Filipino colonialism, to ensure our people's freedom and the preservation of our Islamic and indigenous culture and civilization as well as our revolutionary heritage.

Accordingly, the MNLF declared its intention to work for the restoration of the sovereignty and independence of our people. This declaration was contained in a Manifesto submitted to the 5th Islamic Foreign Ministers Conference in Kuala Lumpur in May 1974.

The "Bangsa Moro Republik" was launched by our people and a revolutionary government was organized at all levels in the liberated areas, complete with its political, military, economic, judicial and other apparatus. Afterwards, a National Parliament and various provincial congresses were enthusiastically organized by our people.

In short a complete state system was brought to life.

MNLF Changes Political Objective and Opts for Political Autonomy

But despite our declaration of intention and largely due to the mediation of the Islamic Conference, the MNLF and our people agreed to tone down our political demand.

Instead of asking, therefore, for complete independence and for the liberation of the entire Bangsa Moro national homeland of Mindanao, Basilan, Sulu and Palawan, which has an aggregate land area of 116,895.3 square kms., the MNLF agreed to put aside its original objective and opted merely for 'complete political autonomy'. While the area we demanded was reduced to 13 provinces and 11 cities, which is roughly 60% of our people's national homeland.

There were other compromises made by the MNLF, as could be seen in the Tripoli Agreement of December 23, 1976 signed by the representatives of the Philippine government, the MNLF, the Quadripartite Ministerial Commission and the Secretary General of the Islamic Conference.

The United Nations, the Organization of the Non-Aligned Countries and the Organization of African Unity have been duly notified about this agreement.

Philippine Colonial Government Sabotages Agreement

But then when the representatives of the Philippine government, the MNLF, the Quadripartite Ministerial Commission, and the Secretary-General of the Islamic Conference met again to flesh up the agreement and prepare the groundworks for its implementation, the Philippine government began to recoil and to put up obstacles in an effort to sabotage what had been formally agreed upon by all the parties concerned.

Two negotiations were held, one in Tripoli last February until March, and the other one in Manila last April. But all our efforts were brought to naught all due to the treachery and betrayal of Marcos and the Philippine colonial government. The MNLF delegation that went to Manila together with the representatives of the Quadripartite Ministerial Commission and the Secretary-General of the Islamic Conference returned empty-handed.

New Phase of the War Starts: Ceasefire is Virtually Scuttled
Following these debacles, the Philippine colonial government intensified its sabotage activities and launched what it called 'a search-and-destroy campaign' against our forces. And yet the joint ceasefire mission, composed of representatives of the Philippine government, the MNLF and the Islamic Conference [was] still in South Philippines actively supervising the implementation of our ceasefire agreement.

As a result of this search-and-destroy campaign, which was launched last July 6, tension rapidly began to mount and last week the second phase of Marcos' war of genocide was commenced. To all intent and purposes and by virtue of this new military campaign of Marcos' colonial armed forces, the ceasefire is virtually over, after 9 months of deceptive peace. South Philippines is therefore once again plunged into a colonial war of genocide. And once again our people are molested and massacred right inside their homes and even in their sacred places as the Tipo-Tipo massacre last August 27 would testify.

And from the look of things, it is impossible to determine how this new war can be stopped.

The Bangsa Moro People Shall Win Final Victory and the MNLF the Final Liquidator of Filipino Colonialism
The Philippine government is pouring in more forces and organizing new paramilitary and terrorist gangs among the colonial settlers. But our people shall remain steadfast and resolute and are decided to carry on with their revolutionary struggle until final victory is achieved and the total liquidation of Filipino colonialism in every part of our people's national homeland shall crown our people's patriotic endeavor. [It is] only then that the Philippine colonial war of genocide against our people and our national culture can be finally stopped.

Now that peaceful solution is impossible with the treacherous and bloodthirsty colonial government of President Marcos, a return to our people's original political objective is at once irresistible and inevitable.

And despite heavy odds, our people and Revolution are certain of their final victory. The final verdict of history shall belong to the Bangsa Moro people and Revolution, and the MNLF and its heroic military arm, the Bangsa Moro Army, shall be the final liquidator and gravedigger of Filipino colonialism in South Philippines.

In this struggle, our people and the MNLF count on the support of all anti-imperialist and revolutionary forces in the world as well as on all other peace-loving peoples of the world.

MNLF Appeals for Unity and Solidarity

Accordingly, and on behalf of the MNLF, I would like to reiterate our appeal to you all and to the peoples of the world to strengthen their unity and solidarity with our people in order to accelerate the momentum of our people's march to final victory and freedom. The victory of our people shall constitute an integral part of the victory of mankind against the forces of colonialism and imperialism in the world.

Once again our thanks to the Lelio Basso Peace Foundation and to the great Algerian People and Government. Thank you.

APPENDIX SEVEN

EXHAUSTIVE SEARCH FOR A PEACEFUL SOLUTION
TO MNLF SECESSION

While the Philippines considers the problem in Southern
Philippines an internal domestic problem, to be resolved
within the framework of the national sovereignty and territorial integrity of the Philippines, it has pursued all peaceful
means of arriving at a just and honorable solution including
direct negotiations, and resort to the good offices of the Islamic
Conference through its Secretary-General and the four-nation
Ministerial Committee.

The Philippine Government agreed to meet with MNLF
representatives on ten occasions from January 1975 to April
1979.

Negotiations and Agreements with MNLF

1. *Jeddah/Tripoli/Cairo/Aswan/Riyadh, January 1975.* Gov-
ernment Panel composed of Executive Secretary Alejan-
dro Melchor, Admiral Romulo Espaldon, Ambassador
Lininding Pangandaman, Ambassador Pacifico A. Cas-
tro, Chancellor Ruben Cuyugan, Dean Cesar Majul,
Col. Jose Almonte, Economist Gary Makasiar, with
MNLF Nur Misuari, Hashim Salamat, Abdul Baki, and
Hasani.

2. *Tripoli, November 1976.* First Lady Mrs. Imelda Romualdez Marcos' meetings with President al-Qadhafi.

3. *Tripoli, December 1976.* Government Panel composed of
Defense Undersecretary Carmelo Barbero, Ambassador
Lininding Pangandaman, Commissioner Simeon Datu-
manong, SPDA Administrator Karim Sidri, Ambassa-
dor Pacifico A. Castro, and Col. Eduardo Ermita with
Nur Misuari, Hashim Salamat, Abdul Baki and Hasani.

   I. Tripoli Agreement of 23 December 1976

4. *Zamboanga City, January 1977.* Admiral Romulo Espaldon with MNLF Commander Tham Manjoorsa.

   II. Cease-fire Agreement of 20 January 1977

5. *Tripoli, February-March 1977.* Government Panel composed of Defense Undersecretary Carmelo Barbero,

Ambassador Pacifico A. Castro, General Paciencio Magtibay, DLGCD Assistant Secretary Ronaldo Puno, and Justice Ministry Counsel Minerva Reyes, with MNLF Nur Misuari, Hashim Salamat, Abdul Baki, Governor Candao and Atty. Balindong.

6. *Tripoli, Benghazi, March 1977.* First Lady Madame Imelda Romualdez Marcos' meetings with Colonel Muammar al-Qadhafi.

   III. Marcos al-Qadhafi Accord of 18–19 March 1977
   IV. Marcos al-Qadhafi Accord of 14 April 1977

7. *Manila, April 1977.* Government Panel composed of Foreign Minister Carlos P. Romulo, Defense Minister Juan Ponce Enrile, Justice Minister Jose Abad Santos, Local Government Minister Jose Rono, Defense Undersecretary Carmelo Barbero, Foreign Undersecretary Manuel Collantes, Ambassadors Pacifico A. Castro and Lininding Pangandaman, Admiral Romulo Espaldon, Major General Fidel Ramos, with MNLF Kagim Jajurie and the Quadripartite Committee (Libyan Foreign Minister Ali Treki, Saudi Political Director Al Khatib, Senegal Ambassador Gaye and Somali Director Darman).

8. *Cairo, January 1973.* Government Panel composed of Ambassadors Jose V. Cruz, Lininding Pangandaman, and Pacifico A. Castro with MNLF Hashim Salamat, Balindong and Hasani.

9. *Cairo, March 1979.* Government Panel composed of Ambassadors Lininding Pangandaman, Pacifico A. Castro and Felino Menez, with MNLF Hashim Salamat, Balindong and Hasani.

10. *Cairo, April 1979.* Government Panel composed of Ambassador Lininding Pangandaman, Abdul Khayer Alonto and Dr. Loong with MNLF Hashim Salamat, Candao and Balindong.

Talks with Nur Misuari's MNLF broke down in April 1977 when MNLF representatives interposed new demands altogether removed from what until then had been the basis of talks with MNLF representatives. The MNLF now wanted a status not contemplated within the unitary constitutional state of the Philippines.

Taking a position different even from the Islamic Conference, the MNLF demanded, among others, formation of a provisional government run exclusively by rebel leaders and the raising by the Philippine Government of a separate army under the sole command of the MNLF. These demands have been overwhelmingly rejected by the people of Southern Philippines, particularly the Muslim communities, which voted against control by the MNLF, in the referendum of April 17, 1977.

With the establishment of the autonomous governments in Regions 9 and 12, the representatives of the autonomous governments have participated in negotiations with MNLF leaders. The speaker of the Legislative Assembly of Region 12, Hon. Abdul Khayer Alonto joined the government panel in meeting with the MNLF group of Hashim Salamat in Cairo.

Much as the Philippines is disposed at any time to have a dialogue with all rebel leaders in self-exile abroad, there has been a delay in the resumption of conversations with the MNLF. Dr. Amadou Karim Gaye, until recently Secretary-General of the Islamic Conference, reported to the Quadripartite Islamic Conference that there is an irreconcilable division in the MNLF leadership, particularly between the groups of Nur Misuari and Hashim Salamat.

The sincerity of the Philippine Government in bringing a better life to Muslims in the Philippines has not been lost among MNLF followers. Today, such MNLF commanders as Hussin Loong, Abdul Khayer Alonto, Hamid Lucman, Nur Naldisa, Al Kaluang, and others are duly elected representatives in the Batasang Pambansa (National Assembly) or the Regional Legislative Assemblies of Regions 9 and 12.

President Marcos has held nine high-level dialogues with representatives of the Islamic Conference:

Dialogues of President Marcos with
Islamic Representatives:

1. *Manila, August 1973.* Meeting with Quadripartite Committee in Malacanang.

2. *Manila, 1974.* Meeting with Secretary-General Mohamed Al Tohamy in Malacanang.
3. *Nairobi, May 1976.* Meeting with Secretary-General Amadou Karim Gaye at the Presidential Suite of Serena Hotel.
4. *Zamboanga City, August 1976.* Meeting with Secretary-General Amadou Karim Gaye and the Quadripartite Committee (Senegal Foreign Minister Assane Seck, Libyan Foreign Undersecretary Abdul Salam Treki and Somali Political Director Darman) at Southcom Headquarters.
5. *Manila, August 1976.* Meeting with Secretary-General Amadou Karim Gaye and the Quadripartite Committee at Malacanang.
6. *Manila, January 1977.* Meeting with Assistant Secretary General Kasim Zuheri.
7. *Manila, April, 1977.* Series of meetings with Secretary-General Karim Gaye and the Quadripartite Committee in Malacanang.
8. *Manila, May 1977.* Meeting with Moroccan Foreign Minister Mohammed Boucetta in his capacity as President of the 10th Islamic Foreign Ministers' Conference.
9. *Manila, February 1980.* Meeting with Islamic Conference Secretary-General Habib Chatti.

In February of 1980, the newly elected Secretary-General of the Islamic Conference, Habib Chatti, visited the Philippines upon the invitation of the Philippine Government. After consultations with President Marcos and a series of meetings with the duly elected representatives of the Muslim communities, the members of the Regional Legislative Assemblies, Secretary-General Chatti promised to help the Philippine Government arrive at a just and honorable peaceful political solution to the MNLF problem, in full respect of the national sovereignty and territory of the Republic of the Philippines.

To inform the countries of the Islamic Conference on the real situation in the Southern Philippines, the Philippines annually sent missions to the Islamic Conferences since 1973:

1. *Benghazi* (4th Islamic Foreign Ministers), 1973. Ambassador Yusup Abubakar.

2. *Kuala Lumpur* (5th Islamic Foreign Ministers), 1974. Ambassadors Lininding Pangandaman and Yusup Abubakar.
3. *Jeddah* (6th Islamic Foreign Ministers), 1975. Ambassador Lininding Pangandaman, General Mamarinta Lao, Commissioner Hashim Abubakar, and Commissioner Datumanong.
4. *Istanbul* (7th Islamic Foreign Ministers), 1976. Ambassadors Rafael Ileto, Lininding Pangandaman, Pacifico A. Castro, and Jose V. Cruz.
5. *Tripoli* (8th Islamic Foreign Ministers), 1977. Ambassadors Rodolfo Tupas and Yusup Abubakar.
6. *Dakar* (9th Islamic Foreign Ministers), 1978. Ambassadors Pacifico Castro, Lininding Pangandaman, and Monico R. Vicente.
7. *New York* (Islamic Foreign Ministers Special Session), 1979. Ambassador Pacifico A. Castro's meetings with outgoing Secretary-General Dr. Amadou Karim Gaye and newly elected Secretary-General Chatti.
8. *Fez, Morocco* (10th), 1979. Ambassadors Pacifico A. Castro and Lininding Pangandaman.
9. *Islamabad, Pakistan* (11th Islamic Ministers), 1980. Ambassadors Pacifico A. Castro and Lininding Pangandaman.

For the same purpose, it sent delegations to related conferences:
1. *Lima* (Nonaligned Foreign Ministers Conference), 1975. Undersecretary Jose D. Ingles, Ambassadors Hortencio Brillantes, Pacifico A. Castro, Alejandro Yango and Counsellor Ernesto Garrido.
2. *Tunis* (Nonaligned Information Ministers Conference), 1976. Public Information Secretary Francisco Tatad and Ambassador Pacifico A. Castro.
3. *Colombo* (5th Nonaligned Summit Conference), 1976. Undersecretary Jose D. Ingles, Ambassadors Hortencio Brillantes, Pacifico A. Castro, Lininding Pangandaman, Alejandro Yango, and Librado Cayco.
4. *Libreville* (10th Organization of African Unity Summit), 1977. Foreign Minister Carlos P. Romulo, Labor Minister Blas Ople, Solicitor-General Estelito Mendoza, Am-

bassadors Pacifico A. Castro, Lininding Pangandaman
and Monico R. Vicente.
5. *Colombo* (Ministerial Meeting of Nonaligned Bureau),
1979. Deputy Minister Jose D. Ingles and Ambassador
Rogelio de la Rosa.
6. *Havana* (6th Nonaligned Summit Conference), 1979.
Deputy Minister Manuel Collantes, Ambassadors Hortencio Brillantes, Pacifico A. Castro and Alejandro
Yango and Counsellor Jaime Yambao.

In September 1976, the Islamic Conference donated $1 mil-
lion to the Muslim communities from the Islamic Solidarity
Fund. This donation was used by the Agency for the Development and Welfare of the Muslims in the Philippines to build
and repair madrasahs and mosques in Mindanao.

The elected representatives of the Muslim communities
have expressed the hope that the Islamic Conference could
play a constructive role in the realization of socioeconomic
projects aimed at normalization of the conditions and the uplift
of the Filipinos in Southern Philippines.

His Excellency, Mr. Carlos P. Romulo,
Minister of Foreign Affairs

SELECTED
BIBLIOGRAPHY
* * *

BOOKS

Filipinas Foundation, Inc. *An Anatomy of Philippine Muslim Affairs: A Study in Depth on Muslim Affairs in the Philippines.* Manila: Filipinas Foundation, 1971.

George, T.J.S. *Revolt in Mindanao: The Rise of Islam in Philippine Politics.* Kuala Lumpur: Oxford University Press, 1980.

Glang, Alunan C. *Muslim Secession or Integration?* Manila: R.P. Garcia, 1969.

Gowing, Peter G., and Robert McAmis, eds. *The Muslim Filipinos.* Manila: Solidaridad Publishing House, 1974.

Gowing, Peter G. *Mandate in Moroland: The American Government of Muslim Filipinos, 1899–1920.* Quezon City: Philippine Center for Advanced Studies, University of the Philippines, 1977.

———. *Muslim Filipinos—Heritage and Horizon.* Quezon City: New Day Publishers, 1979.

Guerrero, Leon Ma. *Encounter of Cultures: The Muslims in the Philippines.* Manila: National Media Production Center for the Department of Foreign Affairs, 1972.

Kiefer, Thomas. *The Tausug: Violence and Law in a Philippine Moslem Society.* New York, 1972.

Mahmoud, Mohammed Fatthy. "Muslims in the Philippines: How They Perceive Their Problems." DPA Dissertation, College of Public Administration, University of the Philippines, 1975.

Majul, Cesar A. *Muslims in the Philippines: Past, Present and Future Prospects.* Pamphlet. Manila: Converts to Islam Society of the Philippines, 1971.

———. *The Historical Background of the Muslims in the Philippines and the Present Mindanao Crisis.* Pamphlet. Marawi City: Ansar ul Islam, 2d National Islamic Symposium, 1972.

———. *Muslims in the Philippines.* 2d ed. Quezon City: University of the Philippines Press, 1973.

———. *Islam and Development: A Collection of Essays.* Manila: Office of the Commissioner of Islamic Affairs, 1980.

Philippine Government. *From Secession to Autonomy: Self-Government in Southern Philippines.* Manila: Ministry of Foreign Affairs, 1980.

ARTICLES

De Los Santos, Joel. "The 'Christian Problem' and the Philippine South." *Asian Studies* (Philippine Center for Advanced Studies, University of the Philippines) 13, no. 2 (August 1975): 27–43.

———. "Towards a Solution of the Moro Problem." *Southeast Asian Affairs 1978.* Singapore: Institute of Southeast Asian Affairs, 1978, pp. 207–214.

Gowing, Peter G. "Muslim Filipinos Between Integration and Secession." *Southeast Asia Journal of Theology* 14, no. 2 (1973): 64–77.

Kiefer, Thomas M. "The Tausug Polity and the Sultanate of Sulu: A Segmentary State in the Southern Philippines." In *Sulu Studies 1*, Gerard Rixhon, ed., pp. 19–64. Jolo: Notre Dame of Jolo College, 1972.

Mahmoud, Mohammad Fatthy. "The Muslims in the Philippines: A Bibliographic Essay." *Asian Studies* (Philippine Center for Advanced Studies, University of the Philippines) 12, nos. 2–3 (August–December 1974): 173–197.

Majul, Cesar A. "Cultural Diversity, National Integration and National Identity in the Philippines." Inauguration Conference of Southeast Asian Social Sciences Association, *Development in Southeast Asia: Issues and Dilemmas.* Hong Kong, 1971.

———. "Some Social and Cultural Problems of the Muslims in the Philippines." *Asian Studies* (Philippine Center for Advanced Studies, University of the Philippines) 14, (April 1976): 83–99.

———. "Towards a Social Policy for the Muslims in the Philippines." *Philippine Political Science Journal* (Philippine Political Science Association) no. 4 (December 1976): 1–17.

Mastura, Michael. "The Moro Problem: An Approach Through Constitutional Reforms." Mimeograph, 1971. 82 pages.

——. "Maguindanao Hopes and Fears from the Constitutional Convention." *Solidarity* 7, no. 4 (April 1972): 18–24.

Moro National Liberation Front, Central Committee, Office of the Chairman. "The Rise and Fall of Moro Statehood: Our Plight and Determination to Survive." Typescript, 1974. 50 pages.

Tamano, Mamimtal A. "How to Solve the Muslim Problem Without Bullets." *Solidarity* 8, no. 6 (December 1973): 17–26.

——. "Suggestions Re-Mindanao Problem." A Memorandum Addressed to President Marcos. Mimeograph, 22 February, 1975. 9 pages.

——. "The Expectations of Muslims as Philippine Citizens." *Solidarity* 10, no. 6 (July–August 1975): 30–34.

INDEX

* * *

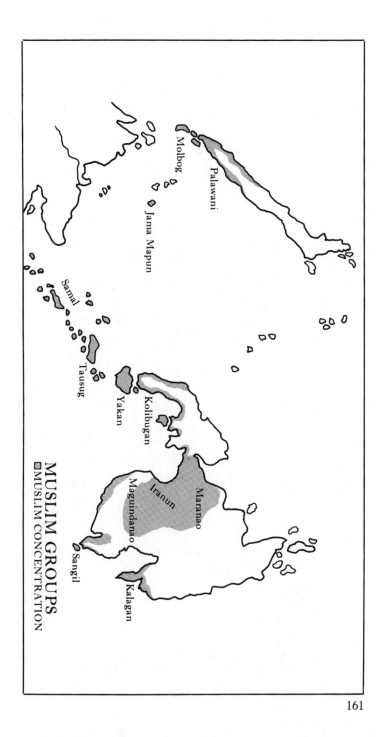

MUSLIM GROUPS
⬛ MUSLIM CONCENTRATION

Molbog

Palawani

Jama Mapun

Samal

Tausug

Yakan

Kolibugan

Maguindanao

Iranun

Maranao

Sangil

Kalagan

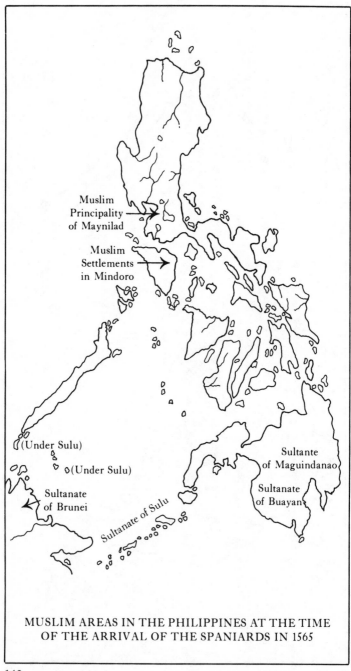

Muslim
Principality
of Maynilad

Muslim
Settlements
in Mindoro

(Under Sulu)

O(Under Sulu)

Sultanate
of Brunei

Sultanate of Sulu

Sultante
of Maguindanao

Sultanate
of Buayan

MUSLIM AREAS IN THE PHILIPPINES AT THE TIME
OF THE ARRIVAL OF THE SPANIARDS IN 1565

ALSO PUBLISHED BY MIZAN PRESS

On the Sociology of Islam: Lectures
Ali Shari'ati
Tr. Hamid Algar

Marxism and Other Western Fallacies: An Islamic Critique
Ali Shari'ati
Tr. R. Campbell

Constitution of the Islamic Republic of Iran
Tr. Hamid Algar

*Islam and Revolution: Writings and Declarations
of Imam Khomeini*
Tr. Hamid Algar

Society and Economics in Islam
Ayatullah Sayyid Mahmud Taleghani
Tr. R. Campbell

The Islamic Struggle in Syria
Dr. Umar F. Abd-Allah

Occidentosis: A Plague from the West
Jalal Al-i Ahmad
Tr. R. Campbell

*Fundamentals of Islamic Thought: God, Man
and the Universe*
Ayatullah Murtaza Mutahhari
Tr. R. Campbell